ORANGE is the new BLACK

PRESENTS

THE COOKBOOK

EDITOR: Samantha Weiner

DESIGNER: Paul Kepple & Ralph Geroni at
Headcase Design, www.headcasedesign.com

PRODUCTION MANAGER: Anet Sirna-Bruder

PROP STYLIST: Sarah Smart

FOOD STYLIST: Christine Albano

Library of Congress Control Number: 2014940778

ISBN: 978-1-4197-1420-7

This book is intended only as an informative
guide for those wishing to know more about
cooking and related issues. Information in
this book is general in nature and is offered
with no guarantees on the part of the authors
or publishers. In no way is this book intended
to replace or conflict with any advice you may
receive from your doctor or other health professionals. The ultimate decision regarding your
health and what you decide to consume should
be made between you and such professionals.
The authors and publisher disclaim all liability
in connection with the use of this book.

WARNING: There may be content contained in this
cookbook that is not suitable for children.

Printed and bound in the United States
10 9 8 7 6 5 4 3 2 1

Abrams Image books are available at special
discounts when purchased in quantity for
premiums and promotions as well as fundraising
or educational use. Special editions can also
be created to specification. For details,
contact specialsales@abramsbooks.com or the
address below.

LIONSGATE®

THE ART OF BOOKS SINCE 1949

115 West 18th Street
New York, NY 10011
www.abramsbooks.com

|ORANGE| is the new |BLACK|

presents

THE COOKBOOK

DEPARTMENT OF JUSTICE

QUI PRO DOMINA JUSTITIA SEQUITUR

FEDERAL DEPARTMENT OF CORRECTIONS

BITES, BOOZE, SECRETS, and STORIES FROM INSIDE THE BIG HOUSE

*by

JENJI KOHAN, TARA HERRMANN, HARTLEY VOSS, and ALEX REGNERY

Recipes by: LEDA SCHEINTAUB * Photographs by: JOHNNY MILLER

ABRAMS IMAGE, NEW YORK

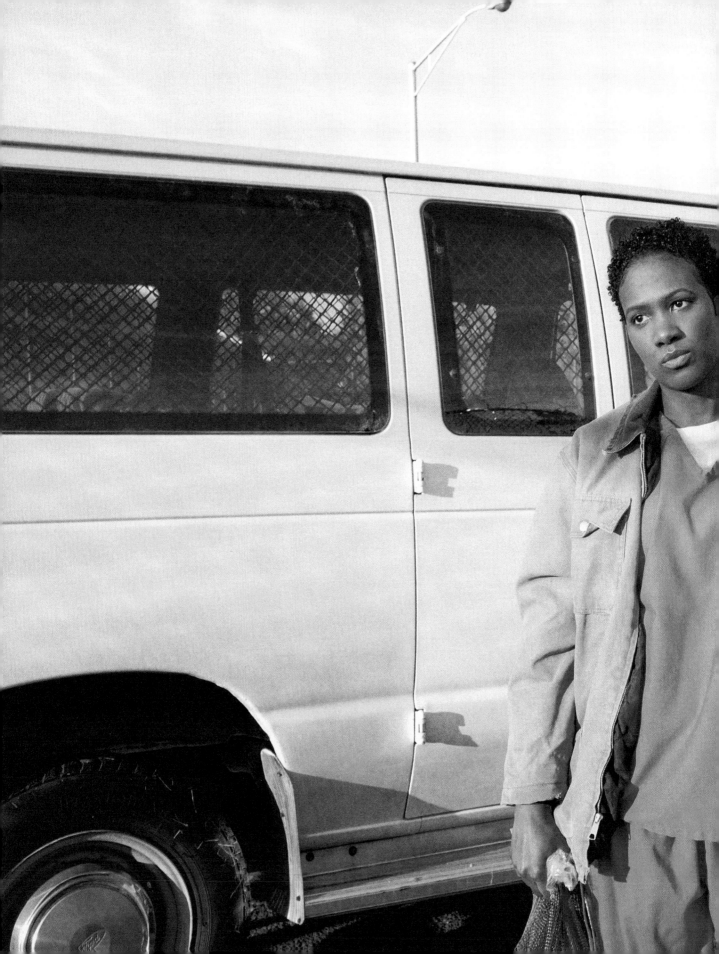

CONTENTS

* *

* * * *

CHAPTER 1: BREAKFAST IN THE BIG HOUSE

* * * *

CHAPTER 2: LUNCH AT LITCHFIELD

* * * *

CHAPTER 3: DINNER IN THE DINING HALL

* * * *

CHAPTER 4: SNACKS AND SIDES FOR SURVIVAL

* * * *

CHAPTER 5: DRINKS IN THE CLINK

* * * *

CHAPTER 6: DESSERT FOR GOOD BEHAVIOR

* * * *

001

BREAK

FAST

IN THE BIG HOUSE

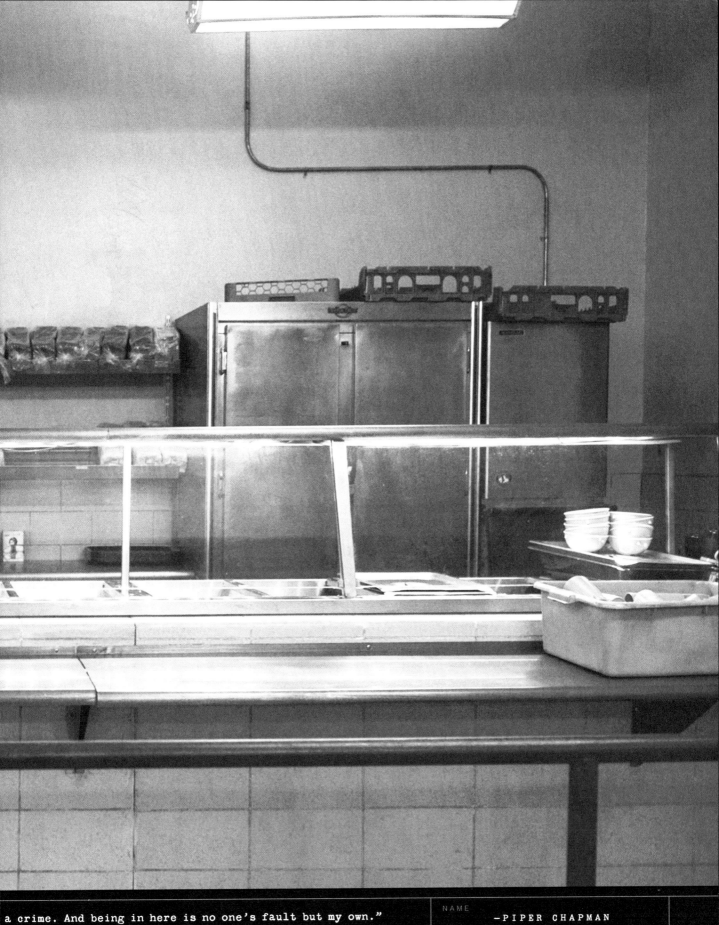

a crime. And being in here is no one's fault but my own."

GLORIA'S CHUNKY OATMEAL

BY............ GLORIA MENDOZA

I'd never run a kitchen before. I never worked in the food service industry, not
even so much as a stint at McDonald's when I was skippin' Mr. Estrada's class. Did
I complain when I was put in charge? Nope. 'Cause it was a hell of a lot better than
grounds crew. Global warming, my ass. Have you seen how cold it gets lately? Just
last year, twenty inches of snow in less than a day. Anyway, it's like pulling off
a holiday dinner three times a day. Learn how to read a few recipe cards, adapt the
recipes with what's in the walk-in, and boss around your girls without being a bitch.
You gotta work with what you got. Otherwise, you're back out in the cold.

SERVES............ 4

INGREDIENTS

¼ teaspoon salt

2 cups (180 g) instant
rolled oats

¾ cup (90 g) raisins

½ teaspoon ground cinnamon

One 5-ounce (147-ml) can
evaporated milk

4 tablespoons (½ stick; 55 g)
unsalted butter

¼ cup (40 g) brown sugar,
plus more for serving

¾ cup (90 g) chopped
toasted walnuts

½ cup (50 g) sweetened
coconut flakes

INSTRUCTIONS

In a medium saucepan, bring the 2½ cups (600 ml) of
water to a boil over high heat and add the salt.
Gradually add the oats, return to a boil, then lower
the heat to medium and cook, stirring, for 1 to 2
minutes, until thickened. Add the raisins and
cinnamon and cook for 1 minute. Add the evaporated
milk and bring to a simmer. Add the butter and brown
sugar and stir until melted. Remove from the heat,
spoon into bowls, and top each serving with brown
sugar, walnuts, and coconut.

POST-PRISON UPGRADE: Substitute chopped dates
for the raisins and replace the evaporated milk with
organic heavy cream.

WAFFLES AND SCRAMBLED EGGS

BY LORNA MORELLO

Sometimes, right before I open my eyes and remember where I am, I like to pretend I'm back in my old life. Breakfast in bed is one of those luxuries couples get to enjoy on the weekends. I liked to sleep in, so Christopher would sneak downstairs and put on a pot of coffee. I'd wake up smelling the aroma, smile, and turn over for a few more minutes of beauty rest. I could hear the eggs gettin' cracked or a sizzling frying pan. It was like a warm blanket for my ears, knowing that the man I loved was making me breakfast. Soon, he'd be coming up the stairs. I'd pretend to still be asleep so he'd think he was the first thing I set eyes on. Fresh flowers, always fresh flowers on the tray. He'd set it on my lap and kiss me. I'd look at my Christopher and think how lucky I am to be marrying such a wonderful man. Time to get up now. They're serving scrambled eggs and waffles, and I'll take what I can get.

SERVES 4 TO 6 (makes about twelve 4-inch/10-cm square waffles, more or less depending on the size of your waffle iron)

INGREDIENTS

WAFFLES

2 cups (300 g) all-purpose flour

2 tablespoons sugar (optional; omit for savory Gloria-style waffles)

1 tablespoon baking powder

½ teaspoon salt

3 large eggs, at room temperature, beaten

1½ cups (360 ml) whole milk, at room temperature

6 tablespoons (85 g) unsalted butter, melted and cooled

Vegetable oil cooking spray

SCRAMBLED EGGS

8 large eggs

Salt and freshly ground white or black pepper

2 tablespoons unsalted butter

INSTRUCTIONS

MAKE THE WAFFLES:

Preheat a waffle iron according to the manufacturer's directions and preheat the oven to 200°F (95°C).

In a medium bowl, whisk together the flour, sugar (if using), baking powder, and salt. In a separate bowl, beat the milk into the eggs, then beat in the butter. Add the wet ingredients to the dry ingredients and whisk until just combined.

Ladle the batter onto the waffle iron according to the manufacturer's directions, spraying it first with cooking spray if necessary. Close the top and cook until the waffles are golden on both sides and are easily removed from the iron. As you make batches of waffles, place them on a baking sheet and keep them warm in the oven until ready to serve.

MAKE THE SCRAMBLED EGGS:

In a large bowl, vigorously beat the eggs together with 1 tablespoon water until light and foamy (adding water makes for fluffy eggs, and it's an ingredient readily available at the commissary), then season with salt and pepper and beat lightly.

WAFFLES AND SCRAMBLED EGGS (cont.)

INGREDIENTS	INSTRUCTIONS
	Melt the butter in a large skillet over medium heat. When the butter starts to bubble, add the eggs. Leave them for about 1 minute, until they begin to set, then using a rubber spatula gently fold the eggs to form billowy curds; continue to fold until the eggs are set but still look fairly wet, another minute or so. Turn off the heat and fold the eggs a few more times.

TO SERVE:

Place the waffles on individual plates, top with the eggs, and serve as is or with the additions in one of the variations below.

VARIATIONS

GLORIA'S SPICY EGGS WITH SALSA: Top your waffles with the scrambled eggs, add a spoonful of jarred salsa, shred a little Jack cheese on top, and drizzle with Rooster Sauce, either homemade (page 119) or store-bought.

POST-PRISON SUNDAY BRUNCH UPGRADE: Substitute whole-wheat flour for half of the all-purpose flour for the waffles and use eggs from free-roaming chickens (occasionally found in the Litchfield yard). Serve with pats of butter, real maple syrup, and crisp farmhouse bacon.

PRISON GLOSSARY

by Lorna Morello

****

WAC . . . . Women's Advisory Council - Ya know, it's when inmates are elected to bring their tribe's concerns to Mr. Healy who in turn speaks to the higher ups, sorta like Student Council.

DOC . . . . Department of Corrections, this one kinda explains itself.

SHU . . . . Solitary Housing Unit - If you been bad, you go to SHU. It's not a place where you want to end up.

Slock . . . . Get yourself a nice long tube sock, stick a combo lock in it and slock away! Your victim will be taking a nap in medical for a long time.

Shiv . . . . It's a prison knife, simple as pie. Sharpen the end of any object and get all stabby with it. Some people call it a "shank," but to each her own!

Nutraloaf . . . . Yuck! Not something you ever want to eat, a mixture of god knows what packed into a loaf-like shape, served in SHU. You're better off eating a shoe.

Bustin' 85 . . . . This is when you gotta have everything in the commissary and you end up spending your maximum amount all at once.

Hooch . . . . Pretty much the only booze you can get in prison. Some people make it in a toilet, but after you've seen the damage these women can do in the bathroom, I'd advise against it. Grab a jar, stick some fruit, condiments and bread, let it sit, and voila!

Chocolate and . . When a white and black inmate do the deed together, Vanilla Swirl sprinkles optional.

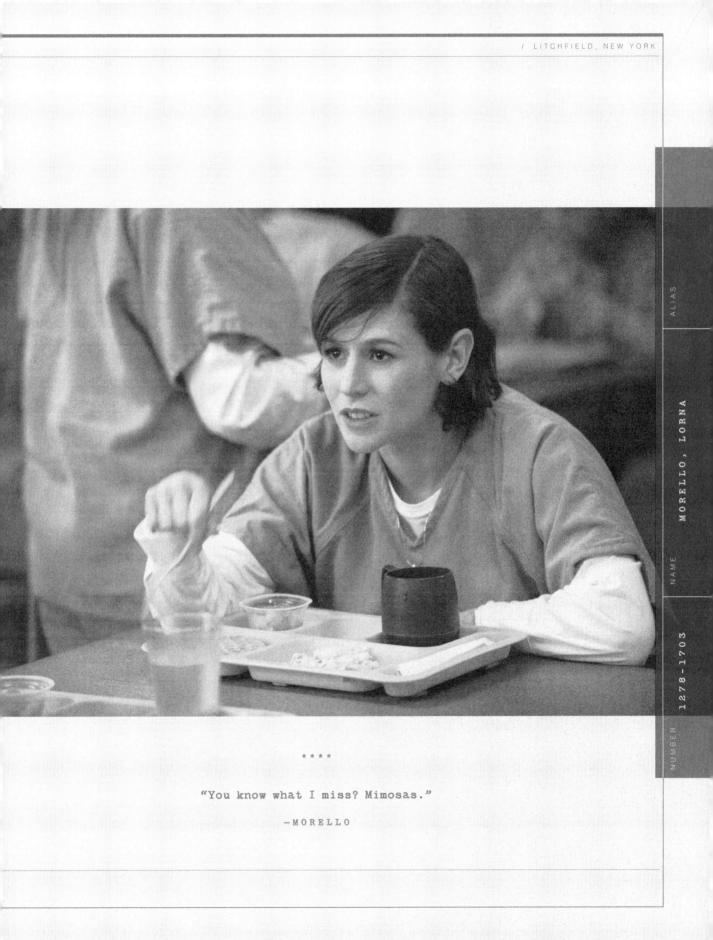

ALIAS

NAME   MORELLO, LORNA

NUMBER 1278-1703

* * * *

"You know what I miss? Mimosas."

—MORELLO

MISS ROSA'S

HUEVOS WITH SPINACH

BY ROSA CISNEROS

Before I came to Litchfield, every Sunday was filled with the scent of a crackling skillet of huevos *and spinach. I can always tell when someone's got good* huevos. *I can see them a mile away. Don't matter if it's a communist in the Universidad de La Habana, a bank teller with a bad haircut, or some little punk walking down Fifth Avenue who don't give a shit what people think of him. If you want the strength to get up and take what's yours in this world, then you gonna want a good breakfast with eggs. The bigger the better.*

SERVES 2

- **2 tablespoons olive oil**
- **2 garlic cloves, pressed through a garlic press**
- **Leaves and tender stems from 1 bunch spinach, washed, well dried, and roughly chopped**
- **4 large eggs**
- **Salt**
- **Toppings: fresh lime juice, fresh or dried oregano, grated Parmesan cheese**

Heat the oil in a medium skillet over medium heat. Add the garlic and let it sizzle for a few seconds. Add the spinach, increase the heat to medium-high, cover, and cook until the leaves reduce in volume and start to wilt, about 2 minutes. Remove the cover and stir the spinach until it is fully wilted and any residual moisture from the leaves has evaporated.

Make four small indentations in the spinach to serve as cooking stations for the eggs. Break an egg into each indentation, cover the skillet, and cook until the whites are set and the yolks are done to your liking, 3 to 5 minutes. Season with salt.

Serve with a squeeze of lime juice, a little oregano, and some Parmesan sprinkled on top. Serve with last night's rice and beans (page 123) if you've got some.

VARIATION

BARE-BONES PRISON VERSION:
Throw some thawed, drained frozen spinach in a pan and heat until bubbling; add the eggs and cook as above. Serve with whatever toppings you can get at.

BREAKFAST SANDWICH (without the tampon)

BY .... ANITA DEMARCO

Waking up attached to a breathing machine surrounded by five other women is not one's ideal situation, but as my nonna said, "Fuggedaboutit." I kid. She said, "Breakfast is the most important meal of the day." I know, so original, but I loved the woman, so step off. Personally, the only way I can get up on my feet is knowing there's a hearty breakfast waiting for me. The prison cafeteria ain't no House of Pancakes, but there's one thing they can't screw up too bad: the timeless breakfast sandwich. Pick your bread. Pick your meat. Pick your sauce. Add an egg and cheese if you want (but none for me, thanks!). Madon! You got a meal that will get you through whatever problems you face, no matter the time. I'd probably eat a breakfast sandwich for every meal in here if I could. And I always make sure to thank the chef. You get on her bad side and it may end up looking like your sandwich was visited by Aunt Flo. Oh!

MAKES .... 2 SANDWICHES

INGREDIENTS

2 short, plump pork sausages, about the length of the buns

1 tablespoon olive oil

Mayonnaise or grainy mustard

2 sandwich buns, split in half and toasted

Red pepper jelly

INSTRUCTIONS

Prick the sausages a few times with a fork and place in a medium skillet. Add the oil and enough water to come a quarter of the way up the sides of the sausages. Place over medium heat and bring to a simmer, then cover and simmer until the sausages are cooked through and the water has evaporated, about 10 minutes. Remove the cover and continue to cook the sausages, turning them a few times, until crisp and well browned on all sides, 3 to 5 minutes. Remove from the pan and split the sausages in half lengthwise.

Spread some mayonnaise on the cut sides of the rolls, place one split sausage cut side facing up on the bottom part of each bun, slather with pepper jelly, and serve.

MY DAILY SCHEDULE

by Sophia Burset

****

4:30 a.m. . . . . . . Shower: You got to be up early to get hot water, clean floors, and space in front of the mirror.

5:00 a.m. . . . . . . Count: I make sure to be back in my bunk in time for the morning inspection.

5:30 a.m. . . . . . Hair Time: My hair has to look perfect before I head out to the cafeteria. That way girls know I can walk the walk when it comes to hairstyles.

6:45 a.m. . . . . . Breakfast: I eat everything I can lay my hands on in the morning. Best way to jump start the metabolism. Pudding, oatmeal, I eat it all.

7:15 a.m. . . . . . Medical Call: The window doesn't open until 7:30 but if I'm late I got to wait behind all the sick girls. They cough and they smell and I don't need none of that.

8:00 a.m. . . . . . Report to Work: I'm supposed to take clients at eight. But girls know not to show up until I've got the place looking good. Unless it's an emergency.

12:00 p.m. . . . . Lunch: I eat quick enough to get a little break before I head back to work. But not so quick that I get gas. It's best when they give out fresh fruit.

4 p.m. . . . . Count: I don't close up till quarter to four, so COs know to count me at the salon. They don't want me rushing out and forgetting a sharp object on the counter.

5 p.m. . . . . Dinner: I eat light at dinner. It's close to bed and my stomach gets upset if I'm not careful. Sometimes I'll just have apple juice if I'm feeling bloated.

7:30 p.m. . . . . . Wheel of Fortune Time: I like to relax in the TV room after working all day. At some point Vanna's gonna retire. I wanna be ready to take over in case they ask.

* * * *

"There's no point in playing shy, baby. You're home."

—SOPHIA

9 p.m. . . . . <u>Count</u>: I look good when the boys come by to check me out. Give them something to think about on their way home at night. Then I'm off to bed.

10 p.m. . . . . . . <u>Lights Out</u>: I'm asleep before the lights go off. I've got to be up early.

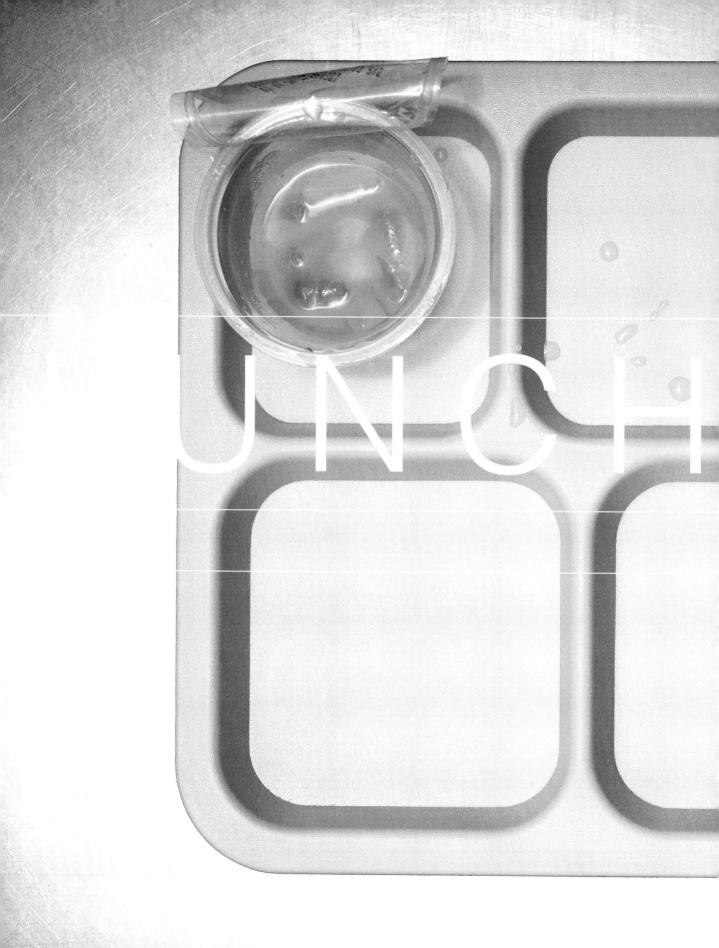

002

AT LITCHFIELD

"...there's the people who serve the bread and the people

who eat the bread."

—GALINA "RED" REZNIKOV

LITCHFIELD
CORRECTIONAL
INSTITUTION

CHAPMAN   PIPER

NAME..
          LAST   FIRST

LIAS..

1278-1945   F   White

NUMBER.. SEX............ RACE..........

NCIC NUMBER

LEAVE BLANK

FINGER PRINT CLASSIFICATION

RIGHT HAND

Index	Middle	Ring	Little

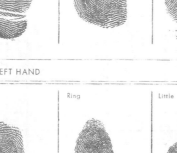

LEFT HAND

Index	Middle	Ring	Little

BURRATA SANDWICH

BY PIPER CHAPMAN

I remember that moment, when all of the sudden it occurred to me, Burrata has swept the nation! You can eat it in a beet salad with baby greens. You can eat it with heirloom tomatoes. You can eat it with habanero pesto. You can drizzle a little olive oil and Maldon salt on it. And if you don't mind the extra carbs, you can put it between two hunks of fresh-baked French baguette. Burrata goes with anything because it's different things to different people. With burrata, your biggest challenge is picking only one option and sticking to it. I love its simple, white freshness. Some people enjoy its creaminess. I guess the truth is that I could go both ways.

MAKES 2 SANDWICHES

- **4 slices country-style white bread or brioche, lightly toasted**
- **8 ounces (225 g) burrata cheese**
- **2 large, thick slices red heirloom tomato**
- **4 slices cooked farmhouse bacon, drippings reserved**
- **Aged balsamic vinegar**
- **Flaky sea salt and coarsely ground black pepper**
- **2 handfuls baby arugula or microgreens**

Place 2 toasted bread slices on a work surface. Spread the burrata on the slices all the way to the edges. Top each with a tomato slice, then drizzle on some bacon drippings followed by a few drops of vinegar. Sprinkle with a little salt and pepper and top with the bacon, followed by the arugula. Cover with the remaining toasted bread slices, press down on them to meld the ingredients, then cut in half and serve.

CRAZY EYES'S DANDELION SALAD

BY . . . . SUZANNE WARREN . . . .

People say they're weeds. People buy poison to kill them. They try to choke them out. Why? By summer's ripening breath this flower may prove a beauteous, delicate, delicious meal, great in a salad after a long canoe trip. Better in a fruit salad after a long game of volleyball. They can do it all! They can grow at the edge of a glamorous golf course sand trap or from the cracks of a broken city sidewalk. To many they are the scourge of a perfect green lawn. But to me they are love. Spread them in the wind, or toss them in a salad.

SERVES . . . . 4 . . . .

INGREDIENTS

DRESSING

3 ounces (85 g) fresh goat cheese, at room temperature

1/3 cup (80 ml) whole milk, plus more if needed

3 tablespoons apple cider vinegar, plus more if needed

SALAD

6 cups (about 250 g) lightly packed torn dandelion leaves

1/2 cup (70 g) raisins, soaked in 1/2 cup (120 ml) white wine or water for 1 hour to plump

1/4 cup (30 g) chopped toasted walnuts

Salt and freshly ground black pepper

INSTRUCTIONS

MAKE THE DRESSING:

In a medium bowl, combine the goat cheese, milk, and vinegar and whisk until smooth and the dressing is a pourable consistency. Add a little more milk if the dressing is too thick.

MAKE THE SALAD:

Place the dandelion leaves in a salad bowl. Add enough dressing to coat (there may be a little dressing left over) and toss well. Add the raisins and walnuts and toss again. Season with salt and plenty of pepper. Taste and add more vinegar if needed to achieve a good balance of bitter, tangy, and sweet. Serve immediately.

VARIATION

Substitute cranberries for the raisins and pecans for the walnuts (based on salad bar availability).

Poem
for Dandelion
By Suzanne Warren

Before I met you,
The sun looked like a
yellow grape.

But now, it looks like fire
in the sky.

Why? Because you light
a fire inside me.

FLACA'S HOLIDAY TAMALES

BY ·
MARISOL "FLACA" GONZALES

Let me tell you, making tamales takes a long-ass time. Like, days, which we don't always got here in lockup. When they first started making them in like Mexico like sixty years ago, they didn't have nothing to do on Christmas Eve except go to church, so no one cared how long it took. But when you got drunk, touchy uncles and loud sisters coming to your tamalada party, trust me, you will want to get the masa ready way in advance. Then you can relax and have fun with everyone around the table singing and smearing that shit on the cornhusks. It's dirty and it gets all over, but at least you can see where everyone's hands are.

MAKES ·
ABOUT 24 TAMALES

INGREDIENTS

TAMALES

One 8-ounce (225-g) package dried cornhusks (see Notes)

$3\frac{1}{2}$ cups (400 g) dried masa harina for tamales (see Notes)

10 ounces (285 g/$1\frac{1}{3}$ cups) pork lard or vegetable shortening, softened

2 teaspoons salt

$1\frac{1}{2}$ teaspoons baking powder

FILLING

$\frac{1}{3}$ cup (25 g) ancho chile powder

1 teaspoon ground cayenne

1 teaspoon ground cumin

1 teaspoon salt, plus more if needed

(continued)

INSTRUCTIONS

PREPARE THE CORNHUSKS:

Put the cornhusks in a large bowl and cover with very hot water. Place a plate on top to keep them submerged and leave for about 2 hours, until the husks are pliable. Choose your cornhusks for making the tamales by sorting through them and taking out 24 of the largest husks; pat them dry with a kitchen towel.

WHILE THE CORNHUSKS ARE SOAKING, MAKE THE FILLING:

Pour $4\frac{1}{2}$ cups (1.1 L) water into a large saucepan and whisk in the ancho chile powder, cayenne, cumin, and salt. Add the meat, place over high heat, and bring to a boil. Partially cover, reduce the heat, and simmer until the meat is fall-apart tender, about 1 hour. Remove the meat with a slotted spoon. Measure out $1\frac{1}{2}$ cups (360 ml) of the broth and set aside to use for the tamales, leaving the rest in the saucepan. Pour $\frac{2}{3}$ cup (150 ml) water into a small bowl and whisk in the masa harina until blended. Raise the heat to medium-high and return the broth to a boil. Strain in the masa mixture and whisk until the mixture comes to a boil and thickens slightly.

INGREDIENTS

1½ pounds (680 g) boneless goat meat (see Notes), cut into 1-inch (2.5-cm) cubes

3 tablespoons dried masa harina for tamales

⅓ cup (40 g) raisins

⅓ cup (40 g) roughly chopped green olives

INSTRUCTIONS

Remove from the heat, taste, and add more salt if needed. Using your fingers or two forks, coarsely shred the meat. Scoop into a bowl and stir in the raisins and olives along with 1 cup (240 ml) of the thickened sauce; add more sauce as needed to thoroughly coat the meat, taste, and season with more salt if needed. Save the rest of the sauce to serve over the tamales.

MAKE THE TAMALE DOUGH:

In a large bowl, combine the masa harina with 2¼ cups (530 ml) hot water. In the bowl of a mixer, combine the lard, salt, and baking powder and beat on medium-high speed until fluffy and light in texture, about 1 minute. Add the masa harina in three additions, beating well after each addition. Reduce the speed to medium-low and add 1 cup (240 ml) of the reserved broth; beat until incorporated. Beat in as much of the remaining ½ cup (120 ml) broth until the dough is the consistency of soft cake batter.

PREPARE THE STEAMER:

Place a penny in the bottom of a deep pot. Set a large colander or steamer basket in the pot and fill the pot with water up to but not touching the basket (so the tamales will be steamed above the simmering water). Line the steamer with a few of the remaining cornhusks, leaving gaps between them so condensing steam can drain off.

FORM THE TAMALES:

Cut twenty-four thin 8- to 10-inch (20- to 25-cm) strips of cornhusks to use for tying the tamales. Lay out one of your chosen cornhusks with the narrower end facing you. Spread about ¼ cup of the dough into about a 4-inch (10-cm) square, leaving at least a 1½-inch (4-cm) border on the side facing you and a ¾-inch (2 cm) border along the other sides. Spoon about 1½ tablespoons of the filling down the center of the

INGREDIENTS

INSTRUCTIONS

dough. Lift up the two long sides of the cornhusk and bring them together so the dough encloses the filling (don't worry if the filling is not completely surrounded with masa; when the masa cooks it will become firm and hold the filling up). Fold up the empty 1½-inch (4-cm) section of the husk and tie one of the strips of husk around the tamal. As you make each tamal, stand it on its folded bottom in the prepared steamer.

STEAM THE TAMALES:

When all the tamales are wrapped and set up in the steamer, cover them with a layer of leftover cornhusks; if there are any gaps in the steamer, fill in the open spaces with some crumpled-up aluminum foil (to keep the tamales from falling over). Cover the pot, place over medium heat, and bring to a simmer. When you hear the penny rattling, you'll know the water is simmering; if the penny stops rattling, the water has boiled away and you'll need to add more water. Cook the tamales for about 1½ hours, then test one: If the husk easily peels away from the masa, it's done. Let the tamales stand in the steamer off the heat for a few minutes to firm up. Warm up the reserved sauce and serve the tamales with the sauce drizzled on top.

NOTES:

Dried cornhusks packaged specifically for tamales are available in Mexican groceries and in the produce or international-foods section of many supermarkets.

Masa harina is a traditional flour made from specially treated corn that is used for making tamales and tortillas (make sure you buy the one marked FOR TAMALES). It is available from Mexican groceries and some supermarkets.

Goat meat is the world's most consumed meat, and it's a staple in Mexican cuisine.

"You called my food disgusting. You're not getting hazed.
You're not getting harassed. You're getting starved. To death!
You'll leave Litchfield as a skeleton in a body bag."

NAME

—RED

* * * *

"There's the Russian woman who runs the kitchen,
totally terrifying, but she takes so much pride in feeding everyone.
You really have to admire the way these women find meaning
in their days. How they take care of each other."

—LARRY BLOOM

RED'S SPICY COMMISSARY TUNA DELIGHT

BY .... GALINA "RED" REZNIKOV ....

When I was in my kitchen at the diner, some of the guys would ask for tuna salad, or
a tuna melt, even though it was not on the menu. There was one Kazak guy who knew I
didn't keep tuna in stock, and still he would always ask. Finally I told him, "Stop
it! There is nothing that stinks more than tuna fish." He told me, "It reminds me of
the sea." "Yuck," I told him. "You're crazy." I hated the stuff. Not even when we had
lines in Soviet Union would I eat tuna. Then I got locked up. The first month I didn't
have my kitchen. I didn't have my friends. When my commissary money came through I
went to stock up and all they had was tuna. I got a can and took it back to my bunk.
I ate it alone and thought of the sea.

SERVES .... 2 ....

INGREDIENTS

One 5-ounce (142-g) can chunk
white tuna in olive oil

2 tablespoons minced celery

2 tablespoons minced carrot

1 scallion, finely chopped

2 to 3 tablespoons mayonnaise,
plus more if needed

1 tablespoon Rooster Sauce,
homemade (page 119) or
store-bought

1 teaspoon fresh lime juice,
or to taste

Salt

Lettuce leaves or 4 slices
crusty bread

INSTRUCTIONS

Put the tuna in a large bowl. Add the celery,
carrot, scallion, mayonnaise, hot sauce, and lime
juice, season with salt, and stir with a fork to
combine, breaking up any large chunks of tuna as you
go. Taste and adjust the consistency and seasonings,
adding more mayonnaise, lime juice, or salt as needed.
Serve over lettuce as a salad or on bread to make
sandwiches.

RED'S HOMEOPATHIC REMEDIES

****

THE COMMON COLD

1)   Drink hot water with honey and butter before going to bed.
2)   Soak legs in hot water up to the knees for 10 to 15 minutes.
3)   Put on wool socks. Get under a warm blanket.
4)   Go to bed.

***   (Not recommended for people suffering a fever.)

SORE THROAT

1)   Add ½ teaspoon salt and ½ teaspoon baking soda to a glass
       of warm water.

***   (Optional addition to mixture: chamomile.)

2)   Gargle. Then spit.
3)   Repeat once every hour or two.

HEADACHE

1)   Grate 2 lemons.
2)   Gently massage temples (or affected area) with the lemon zest
       for 5 minutes.
3)   Drink green tea laced with mint leaves.

KEEP A BURN FROM SCARRING

1)   Mix some lemon juice with Vaseline, apply it every day.

TO GET RID OF PLANT FUNGUS

1)   Use a mixture of garlic, vinegar, and hot pepper sauce. It's a
       natural insecticide.

RED'S TUNNEL SUPPLY LIST

* *

If your son is tunneling into your prison, here are some things you should
tell him to bring:

*   Dark, secondhand clothing that won't attract attention and can be
    thrown out after getting dirty.
*   A small battery-operated fan to leave on at the entrance to the
    tunnel blowing fresh air inside.
*   A headlamp.
*   A small, portable welding torch, which can be ordered online.
*   A welding mask.
*   Workman's gloves.
*   A watch.
*   Bottled water.
*   A backpack to carry all the above items.

* * * *

"I'm missing half my zucchini...I'm all out of

cucumbers, carrots, beets.

God knows what they're doing with those."

—RED

LITCHFIELD
CORRECTIONAL
INSTITUTION

NAME..... PARKER   YVONNE
         LAST   FIRST

ALIAS..... Vee

NUMBER..... 1973-1101   SEX.... F   RACE.... Black

NCIC NUMBER

LEAVE BLANK

FINGER PRINT CLASSIFICATION

RIGHT HAND

mb	Index	Middle	Ring	Little

LEFT HAND

mb	Index	Middle	Ring	Little

VEE'S

BUTTERNUT SQUASH, LEEK & GINGER SOUP

BY YVONNE "VEE" PARKER

I taught myself to cook. No home ec in high school or an Easy-Bake Oven when I was little. Being on your own, you learn what's simple and filling. Soups are something I find comfort in, since it doesn't get much easier than throwing things in a pot and letting them stew. I can still picture a simmering pot of my homemade broth—a warm bath for your belly. Taking in a bunch of kids—running my own island of misfit toys, if you will—doesn't make my life any easier. But if I always have a soup on the stove, they're fed, they're happy, and they know who takes care of them. Where would they be without me? Nowhere good, that's where.

SERVES 4 TO 6

- **One 3½-pound (1.5-kg) butternut squash, peeled, cut in half lengthwise, seeds and fibrous threads removed, flesh cut into 1-inch (2.5-cm) chunks**
- **5 tablespoons olive oil, divided**
- **3 tablespoons balsamic vinegar, plus more if needed**
- **Salt and freshly ground black pepper**
- **2 tablespoons unsalted butter**
- **2 large leeks, white and light green parts only, chopped and washed thoroughly (reserve the greens for Grab Everything You Can Carry Leek Stock; see opposite)**
- **2 tablespoons minced fresh ginger**
- **½ teaspoon ground turmeric**
- **2 tablespoons white wine**
- **6 cups (1.5 L) Grab Everything You Can Carry Leek Stock (recipe follows) or store-bought vegetable stock**
- **¼ to ½ cup (60 to 120 ml) heavy cream (optional)**
- **½ cup (120 ml) sour cream (optional)**
- **½ cup roasted salted pumpkin seeds (optional)**

Preheat the oven to 425°F (220°C) and line a baking sheet with parchment paper or aluminum foil.

Place the squash in a large bowl, add 3 tablespoons of the oil, the vinegar, 1 teaspoon salt, and lots of pepper. Toss to coat the squash, then arrange the squash pieces on the prepared baking sheet in a single layer. Place in the oven and roast for about 45 minutes, turning a couple of times, until softened and browned at the edges. Remove from the oven and set aside.

In a large saucepan, melt the butter in the remaining 2 tablespoons oil over medium heat (you can get started on this once the squash is about halfway through roasting). Add the leeks and cook, stirring occasionally, until very soft and lightly colored, about 10 minutes. Add the ginger and cook for about 5 minutes, until softened. Add the turmeric and cook for 1 minute.

Add the wine and stir to release any browned bits from the bottom of the pan. Add the roasted squash (it's OK if it's still hot from the oven) and stock and increase the heat to medium-high. Bring to a simmer, then reduce the heat to low, cover, and simmer for 15 minutes to combine the flavors. Working in batches, puree the soup in a blender until smooth. Return the soup to the pan and add the cream, if using. Add more stock or some water if the soup is too thick. Season with salt and pepper and add some more vinegar if you feel it needs a hit of acid. Serve, topped with sour cream and roasted pumpkin seeds if you've got them.

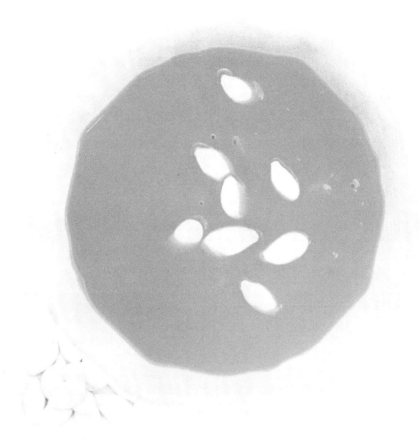

GRAB EVERYTHING YOU CAN CARRY LEEK STOCK

MAKES 6 CUPS (1.5 L)

- **2 large leeks, green parts only, washed thoroughly**
- **Optional additions: 1 chopped carrot, 1 chopped onion, 2 smashed garlic cloves, handful of whole black peppercorns**

In a large saucepan, combine all the ingredients with 6¼ cups (1.6 L) water. Place over medium-high heat, cover, and bring to a boil. Reduce the heat to low and cook at a low simmer for 45 minutes. Strain into a bowl, pressing on the vegetables to extract all the liquid; discard the solids. Use the stock immediately, or let cool, transfer to a container, and store in the refrigerator, where the stock will keep for up to 5 days.

HEALY'S MOM'S
MUSHROOM BARLEY SOUP

BY SAM HEALY

All through elementary school, my lunch box consisted entirely of a Thermos. Other kids received sandwiches with the crusts cut off and notes with hearts over the "i"s but that wasn't the case for me. Mother was best at making soups. The portions were plentiful and the prep was easy for a woman who took a few minutes to cut a carrot. On the weekends, I'd stand at the sink, peeling vegetables and handing them off to her as she stared out the window, listening to Have Gun— Will Travel on the radio. Sometimes I'd peel a little too fast and she would get flustered, so I'd hold her hand and give her a smile. She'd smile back, take a breath, and get back to chopping.

Before the summer when Father took her away, that woman made the most delicious roasts and pasta primavera. Mother returned home in August, and with her came the stews and bisques and creams of whatever vegetable was in the house. Every day at school, the kids around me would be trading off snacks. Potato chips for a pudding. Cookies for a cupcake. I'd unscrew the top of my Thermos and pour a cup of piping hot soup. None of the kids asked to trade, but I wouldn't have traded Mother's soup for anything.

SERVES 4

- **3 tablespoons extra-virgin olive oil**
- **1 medium onion, finely chopped**
- **2 medium carrots, finely chopped**
- **2 celery ribs, finely chopped**
- **4 garlic cloves, finely chopped**
- **1 pound (455 g) white button or cremini mushrooms, thinly sliced**
- **Salt**
- **1 tablespoon dried dill**
- **¼ cup (60 ml) dry sherry**
- **6 cups (1.5 L) beef, chicken, or vegetable stock**
- **½ cup (100 g) pearled barley**
- **Freshly ground black pepper**
- **2 tablespoons fresh lemon juice, or to taste**
- **½ cup (15 g) chopped fresh dill, plus more for garnish**
- **Sour cream or crème fraîche (optional)**

Heat the oil in a large saucepan over medium heat. Add the onion, carrots, and celery and cook until softened, about 5 minutes. Add the garlic and cook for about 2 minutes, until softened. Add the mushrooms and a pinch of salt to help bring the liquid out of the mushrooms and cook, stirring often, until the mushrooms are very soft, release their liquid, and the liquid evaporates, about 15 minutes. Add the dried dill and cook for about 1 minute, until aromatic. Add the sherry and cook until evaporated, about 2 minutes. Add the stock and barley, season with salt and pepper, and bring to a boil. Reduce the heat to low, cover, and cook, stirring occasionally, until the barley is softened, about 30 minutes. Stir in the lemon juice and season with more salt and pepper if needed. Stir in the fresh dill and serve, with more fresh dill and sour cream as a garnish if you like. Serve with good crusty bread.

"Lesbian request denied."

NAME	
	—SAM HEALY

BLANCA'S CHICKEN ENCHILADAS (with Chipotle Tomatillo Sauce)

BY .... BLANCA FLORES (Translated from Spanish)

I push the limits in life. When my mom told me she'd kick me out of the house if I wore a skirt above my knee, I wore one that barely covered my ass. When my cousin told me she don't like tickling, I tied her up and tickled her till she was crying. When Diablo said he doesn't like my bush shaved, I got it waxed. When my lawyer said I would go to prison if I didn't take the plea, I ended up here. So when I was five and my sister dared me to drink an entire can of enchilada sauce what do you think I did? Yeah. But you know the funny thing? I loved it.

SERVES .... 4 TO 6

INGREDIENTS

2 pounds (910 g) bone-in chicken thighs

Salt

2 cups (6 ounces/170 g) shredded Monterey Jack cheese

2 pounds (910 g) tomatillos

2 unpeeled garlic cloves

½ bunch fresh cilantro, leaves and stems, plus additional leaves for garnish

1 teaspoon ground chipotle chile

Twelve 6-inch (15-cm) corn tortillas

Sour cream

(continued)

INSTRUCTIONS

Put the chicken thighs in a large saucepan. Add cold water to just cover the chicken and season with salt. Cover the pan, place over high heat, and bring to a boil. Reduce the heat to low and simmer, uncovered, for 10 minutes. Turn off the heat, cover the pan, and let stand until the chicken is no longer pink in the center, about 30 minutes. Remove the chicken from the pan using tongs or a slotted spoon and place on a plate. Measure out ½ cup (120 ml) of the broth and set aside; reserve the rest for another use (such as Healy's Mom's Mushroom Barley Soup on page 53). Let the chicken cool, then remove the skin and pull the meat from the bones. Shred the chicken using your hands or two forks, then chop it into bite-size pieces. Put the chicken in a large bowl, add some of the reserved broth—up to ¼ cup (60 ml)—just enough to moisten the chicken, and add 1½ cups (4½ ounces/125 g) of the cheese. Season with salt.

While the chicken is poaching, preheat the broiler. Remove the papery husks and stems from the tomatillos, wash them well, and dry them. Place them on a

INGREDIENTS

INSTRUCTIONS

broiler pan along with the garlic cloves and broil
for about 10 minutes, turning them after 5 minutes,
until blackened all over. Remove from the broiler
and set the oven to 450°F (230°C).

Peel the garlic and place the tomatillos and garlic
in a food processor. Add the remaining reserved ¼
cup (60 ml) chicken broth, the cilantro, chipotle,
and 1 teaspoon salt and pulse several times until
all the ingredients are blended into a chunky
sauce. Pour into a bowl, taste, and add more salt
if needed.

Heat a medium skillet over medium heat. Place
1 tortilla on the skillet and heat for about 20
seconds on each side, until pliable but not
colored. Repeat with the remaining tortillas,
stacking them as you go.

Line the bottom of a 9-by-13-inch (23-by-33-cm)
baking dish with ¾ cup (180 ml) of the tomatillo
sauce. Spread about ⅓ cup of the filling down the
center of each tortilla. Roll each tortilla loosely
and place in the baking dish, seam side down. Pour
the remaining tomatillo sauce over the top of the
enchiladas, spreading it with a rubber spatula to
evenly coat all the tortillas. Sprinkle with the
remaining ½ cup (1½ ounces/45 g) of the cheese and
cover the baking dish with foil. Place in the oven
and bake for about 20 minutes, until the enchiladas
are heated through and the cheese is melted. Uncov-
er, sprinkle with cilantro, and serve, with sour
cream on the side for folks to take a dollop.

INMATES WHO DOUBLE
BACK THROUGH THE
SERVICE LINE AND RECEIVE
PORTIONED ITEMS WILL
RECEIVE AN INCIDENT
REPORT.

EXCHANGING FOOD
ITEMS FROM ONE
PERSON TO ANOTHER IS
NOT PERMITTED ON THE
SERVING LINE.

003

INNE

R

IN THE DINING HALL

"Feeding an entire prison population day in and day out is a whole

MARITZA'S MEXICAN ELECTION PIZZA

BY .... **MARITZA RAMOS**

I learned to make pizza from a fat, sweaty busboy at a restaurant in Boston. He wanted to impress me and he didn't have any money or nothing. Most guys, they know I like riding in expensive cars and drinking on airplanes. One guy bought me a bling-covered flatiron, 'cause he knew how much I love to straighten my hair and he thought it would get him somewhere with me. Another guy asked me to marry him in skywriting with purple smoke, my favorite color. But this busboy from Boston took me to the back of the restaurant and showed me how to make the most amazing pizza I ever had. It was more romantic than a hundred ponies with golden horseshoes and diamond collars. I just know it's going to win me that spot on WAC.

MAKES .... **ONE 12-INCH (30-CM) PIZZA**

INGREDIENTS

One 12-inch (30-cm) fresh or frozen pizza shell

8 ounces (225 g) ground beef

½ small red onion, finely chopped

2 garlic cloves, minced

¼ teaspoon dried oregano

Salt

Half 16-ounce (454-g) can refried beans

1 cup (240 ml) prepared salsa, drained slightly if watery

4 ounces (115 g) Monterey Jack cheese, shredded (about 1 cup)

1 scallion, thinly sliced

One 4.5-ounce (127-g) can chopped green chiles, drained

INSTRUCTIONS

Preheat the oven according to the instructions on your pizza shell.

Put the ground beef in a medium skillet, place over medium heat, and cook, stirring often to break up any lumps in the meat, until browned with no pink spots remaining, about 10 minutes. Add the onion, garlic, and oregano and cook until the onion and garlic are softened, about 5 minutes. Season with salt, remove from the heat, and let cool.

Spread the refried beans over the pizza shell and top with the beef. Spoon the salsa evenly on top. Distribute the cheese over the pizza, place in the oven, and bake according to the instructions on your pizza shell, until the crust is crisp and the cheese is bubbling. Remove from the oven, sprinkle with the scallion and green chiles, cut into slices, and serve.

VEGETARIAN VARIATION: Skip the beef.

LARRY'S
ORANGE & BLACK PEPPERCORN
PULLED PORK

BY LARRY BLOOM

Pork. The other white meat. Or as my mother called it, the "not in my house" meat. For years I was deprived of the joys of pork chops and applesauce, crisp bacon and baby back ribs. I had a little run-in with high cholesterol in college when I had to have a plate of bacon to cure my hangovers. When the doctor told me what my LDLs were, my mom nearly had a heart attack (yes, my mom was there; like your mom never took you to the doctor when you were home from college). I learned how to eat pork responsibly, and it plays an important (yet slightly smaller) role in my life to this day.

SERVES 6 TO 8

- 2 tablespoons achiote powder (see Note)
- 4 garlic cloves, pressed through a garlic press
- 1½ tablespoons whole black peppercorns, lightly crushed
- 2 tablespoons finely chopped fresh oregano, or 2 teaspoons dried oregano
- 2 teaspoons salt, plus more if needed
- ¼ cup (60 ml) fresh orange juice
- ¼ cup (60 ml) fresh lime juice, plus more to taste
- 2 tablespoons apple cider vinegar
- One 3-pound (1.3 kg) boneless pork shoulder
- Warm corn tortillas
- Optional garnishes: chopped fresh cilantro leaves, jalapeño slices, diced white onion, lime wedges

In a medium bowl, make the marinade by combining the achiote powder, garlic, peppercorns, oregano, and salt. Whisk in the orange juice, lime juice, and vinegar.

Place the meat in a heavy-duty zip-top bag, add the marinade, seal the bag, and massage the paste all over the meat. Cover and refrigerate for at least 8 hours or overnight.

Thirty minutes before you're ready to roast, preheat the oven to 300°F (150°C) and take the meat out of the refrigerator.

Place the meat in a large oven-safe pot and drizzle the marinade on top. Pour 1 cup (240 ml) water around the meat, cover tightly, and roast for about 3½ hours, until fall-apart tender, checking the pot occasionally and adding more water if the liquid level runs low. Place meat on a carving board and pour the juices into a gravy separator or liquid measuring cup. Let the meat cool slightly, then shred it and return it to the roasting pot. Spoon off as much of the fat from the juices as you like and pour as much of the fat and marinade back into the meat as needed to liberally moisten it; pour the rest into a saucepan and keep warm over low heat. Taste the meat and add more salt and lime juice if needed. Cover the pan and keep warm on the stovetop over low heat until ready to serve. Serve scooped into corn tortillas with juices drizzled on top along with your choice of toppings.

NOTE: *Achiote, also known as annatto, is a seed that lends an orange-hued color to dishes. It can be found, either in whole seed form or ground, in Latin American markets.*

```
                         * * * *

TAYSTEE:  Let's talk about health
          care, Mackenzie.
POUSSEY:  Oh, Amanda, I'd rather
          not. It's not polite.
TAYSTEE:  Did you see that
          wonderful new documentary
          about the best sushi in
          the world? Of course, now
          that I'm vegan, I didn't
          enjoy it as much as I
          might have before.
POUSSEY:  You know, I just don't
          have the time. Chad and
          I have our yoga workshop,
          then wine-tasting class,
          and then we have to have
          really quiet sex every
          night at nine.
TAYSTEE:  Did you hear that piece
          on NPR about hedge funds?
POUSSEY:  Amanda, let me ask you,
          what do you think about
          my bangs these days? I
          mean, do you like them
          straight down, or should
          I be doing more of a
          sweep to the side?
TAYSTEE:  Sweep to the side.
```

MACKENZIE AND AMANDA'S VEGAN SUSHI

BY......... **MACKENZIE AND AMANDA WHITEPERSON**

When we finish up at one of our many charity events, we're usually famished and re-
quire a smart, sensible, yet worldly meal to get us through the first installment of
Wagner's Ring Cycle at the Met. The refrigerator is empty because the housekeeper was
busy picking up little Nicole at her piano recital, and heaven knows we'd never cook
for ourselves. Isn't that what a restaurant is for? Oh, that reminds us: We read the
most devastating piece in the New Yorker about overfishing. It made us rethink our
entire stance on all fish products. There's nothing that says we are humble and whole
like some vegan sushi. Maybe we'll get really crazy and put some wasabi on our roll.

MAKES......... **3 ROLLS (24 TO 30 PIECES)**

INGREDIENTS

1 cup (200 g) sushi rice

2 tablespoons rice vinegar

1 teaspoon sugar

½ teaspoon fine salt

3 sheets roasted nori seaweed

3 teaspoons umeboshi paste
(see Notes)

½ medium cucumber, peeled,
cut in half horizontally,
seeds scraped out, and cut
into about 8-by-¼-inch
(20-cm-by-6-mm) lengthwise
strips (just a little shorter
than the length of the long
side of the nori)

½ avocado

Fresh lemon juice

Soy sauce, wasabi, and pickled
ginger

(continued)

INSTRUCTIONS

Put the rice in a fine-mesh strainer and rinse under
the tap for about 1 minute, until the water runs
clear. In a large saucepan, combine the rice with
1¼ cups (300 ml) water. Place over high heat, bring
to a boil, then reduce the heat to low, cover, and
simmer for about 15 minutes, until the water is
absorbed and the rice is tender. Remove from the heat
and let the rice stand, covered, for 10 minutes.

Meanwhile, in a small bowl, combine the vinegar,
sugar, and salt. Stir it a few times while your rice
is cooking to dissolve the sugar and salt.

Dump the rice into a large bowl and pour the vinegar
mixture over it. Using a large spatula and a fan (a
piece of cardboard can work as a stand-in), fold the
vinegar into the rice while fanning the mixture to
cool it down to room temperature.

Place a sheet of nori shiny side down on a bamboo
rolling mat (see Notes) with a long side facing
you. Fill a small bowl with water and have it handy.
Wet your hands and spread one third of the rice
(about ¾ cup/125 g) evenly over the nori sheet,
leaving a 1-inch (2.5-cm) border at the far end.

INGREDIENTS

INSTRUCTIONS

Lightly press on the rice so it sticks to the sheet. Wet your hands anytime the rice starts sticking to them, but take care not to get the nori wet to keep it from getting soggy.

Spread 1 teaspoon of the umeboshi paste over the rice in a ½-inch (12-mm) or so horizontal strip over the bottom of the sheet of rice-covered nori. Arrange one third of the cucumber strips over the umeboshi paste. Peel and pit the avocado, rub it with lemon juice, and cut it into strips ¼ inch (6 mm) thick. Arrange some of the avocado strips on top of the cucumber strips. Hook your thumbs below the bamboo mat and roll the edge up and over the filling, using your fingers as a guard to keep the filling from falling out. Continue rolling, being careful not to roll the mat along with the sushi. When you've reached the end, give the roll a nice squeeze from all around to shape it.

Trim the ends of the roll and cut the roll with a sharp knife into 8 to 10 pieces. Serve the rolls with tiny dishes of soy sauce, a schmear of wasabi, and a few slices of pickled ginger.

NOTES:

Umeboshi is a salty, sour pickled plum with an assertive pucker-your-mouth quality; it's used widely as a seasoning in Japanese cuisine.

Bamboo sushi mats are available at Japanese groceries, good supermarkets in the international-foods section, and online; if you don't have one, try substituting a sheet of plastic wrap or a tea towel or just roll it sans mat with a firm yet gentle hand to ensure the filling stays secure without tearing the nori.

NAME........ DOGGETT   TIFFANY
                    LAST   FIRST

NUMBER........ 1499-5190   SEX.... F   RACE.... White

Pennsatucky

BEER CAN BIRD

BY TIFFANY "PENNSATUCKY" DOGGETT

My mama's brother's daddy Marvin was the inventor of the beer can bird, although no one give him credit for it and everyone says he stole it from his stepsister Susie. Back then beer cans was bigger and he'd have to really shove it up there hard. That's what they tell me, anyway. He passed before I was born. I do remember the first time my uncle served me some of his beer bird. We were out on the fall hunting trip when I was five— deeeelish. 'Course, he was more of an Old Milwaukee man and everybody knows a good can of Bud is the way to go. But he was from a different generation. They didn't know about things like that back then.

MAKES 1 BIG-ASS TURKEY

RUB:

- **2 teaspoons dry mustard powder**
- **2 teaspoons smoked paprika**
- **1 teaspoon garlic powder**
- **1 teaspoon onion powder**
- **1 teaspoon dried thyme**
- **1 teaspoon dried oregano**
- **1 teaspoon ground cumin**
- **1 teaspoon freshly ground black pepper**
- **2 teaspoons salt**
- **½ teaspoon ground cayenne**

- **One 12- to 14-pound (5.5- to 6.25-kg) free-range turkey**
- **1 medium chunk of smoking wood, such as apple wood**
- **One 24- or 25-ounce (740-ml) can of beer**

Fire up a smoker or grill to 325°F (160°C) on one side.

MAKE THE RUB:

In a small bowl, combine all the rub ingredients.

Remove and discard the neck and giblets from the turkey. Rinse the turkey under cold water and pat dry with paper towels. Rub the cavity with about 1 tablespoon of the rub. Using your fingers, gently separate the skin from the meat underneath the breasts and around the thighs. Spread about 1 tablespoon of the rub under the breast and thighs. Open the beer can and pour yourself about one third of the beer. Make a few more openings in the can using a can opener and leave the rest of the beer in the can. Add about 1 tablespoon of the rub to the beer can. Sprinkle the remaining rub into the cavity of the turkey and all over the turkey, inserting it under the skin.

When the grill comes up to temperature, add the wood chunk. When the wood ignites and starts to smoke, place the beer can on the grill over the unheated portion. Carefully lower the turkey onto the beer can, legs down. Adjust the legs so the bird is stable on the grill. (If it's hard to get it to stay stable, you could place the bird, beer in butt, in a roasting pan before placing it on the grill.) Cover and smoke until an instant-read thermometer registers 160°F (70°C) in the thickest part of the breast, 2 to 3 hours.

Remove the turkey from the smoker, place it on a carving board, and let it rest for about 20 minutes. Remove the beer can, carve, and serve.

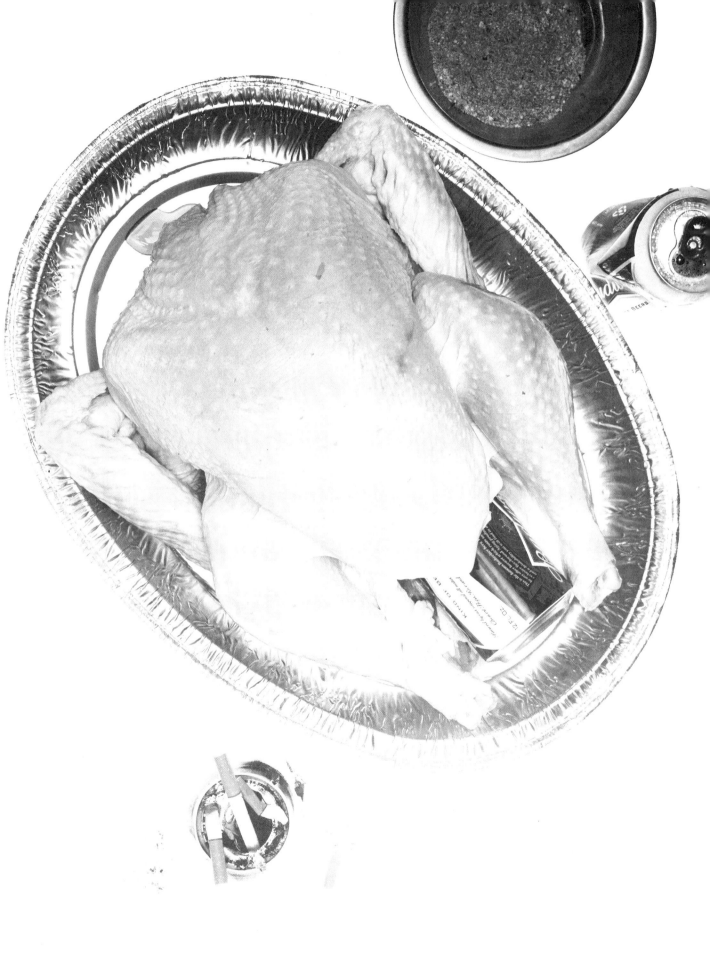

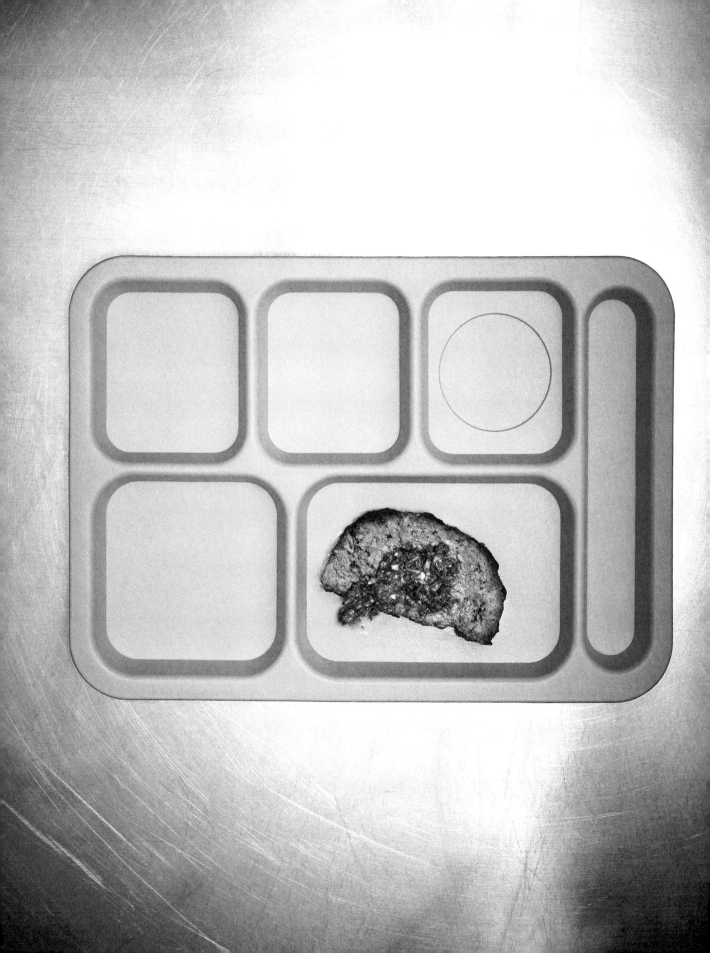

SHU MOLDY MYSTERY MEAT

FROM..................
THE DOC DIETARY INFORMATION PAMPHLET

The Department of Corrections provides all of its inmates with a well-balanced and nutritional diet. When sequestered to the SHU, inmates are given three meals a day, based on the dietary parameters from lead nutritionists in the field. These nutritionists consult with our headquarters kitchen staff to come up with healthy, delicious, and cost-effective meal plans. With one bite of our specialized SHU meal, you'll be saying, "Mmm! What is this?" But that's one secret we'll never tell.

SERVES.................. 6

INGREDIENTS

MEATLOAF

2 tablespoons olive oil

1 large onion, finely chopped

Leaves from 1 bunch spinach, chopped

2 tablespoons grated lemon zest

2 pounds (910 g) ground beef

1 cup (55 g) panko breadcrumbs

1 large egg

1 large egg white

1 teaspoon ground cumin

2 teaspoons salt

½ teaspoon freshly ground black pepper

(continued)

INSTRUCTIONS

MAKE THE MEATLOAF:

Preheat the oven to 350°F (170°C) and set up a broiler pan with the drip pan placed on top. Take the beef out of the refrigerator 30 minutes before you're ready to bake the meatloaf (this makes it easier to work the ingredients into it).

Heat the oil in a large skillet over medium heat. Add the onion and cook until softened, about 5 minutes. Increase the heat and add the spinach; cook until the spinach is wilted and most of the liquid that's released is evaporated, about 3 minutes. Remove from the heat, stir in the lemon zest, spread over a large plate or cookie sheet, and let cool.

In a large bowl using your clean hands (or wearing disposable gloves), gently combine the ground beef, breadcrumbs, and cooled spinach mixture. In a separate bowl, whisk the egg with the egg white, then whisk in the cumin, salt, and pepper. Add to the meat mixture and combine lightly (don't mash it or the loaf may turn out dense). On the broiler pan, form the meat into a rectangular loaf that's about

SHU MOLDY MYSTERY MEAT (cont.)

INGREDIENTS

CHIMICHURRI SAUCE

1 cup (35 g) packed fresh parsley leaves

1 cup (35 g) packed fresh mint leaves

2 tablespoons fresh oregano leaves (optional)

1 large shallot, finely chopped

4 garlic cloves, finely chopped

½ cup (120 ml) olive oil

2 tablespoons red wine vinegar

½ teaspoon salt, or to taste

¼ teaspoon red chile flakes, or to taste

INSTRUCTIONS

9 inches (23 cm) long, 4 inches (10 cm) wide, and 3 inches (7.5 cm) high.

Place in the oven and bake for about 1 hour, until a meat thermometer reads 160°F (70°C) and the meat is cooked through. Remove from the oven and set aside to rest for 10 minutes.

WHILE THE MEATLOAF IS RESTING, MAKE THE CHIMICHURRI SAUCE:

Combine the parsley, mint, oregano, if using, shallot, and garlic in a food processor and pulse until finely chopped but not pureed, stopping and scraping the sides of the bowl with a rubber spatula once or twice, about 1 minute total.

Transfer the mixture to a large bowl and stir in the oil and vinegar. Season with the salt and red chile flakes. Slice the meatloaf, place it on plates, and serve with the chimichurri sauce on top.

"Did you get this loaf thing? Looks like three different dinners mushed into a mound."

NAME

—PIPER

RED'S
CHICKEN KIEV

BY GALINA "RED" REZNIKOV

No one in Kiev gives two shits about their famous dish of poultry. I went there as a student. I asked at the hotel, "Where is the best chicken Kiev?" But when I took their advice, the restaurant was a joke. They put mayonnaise and ketchup on the bird. No. Keep it simple. All you need is a little flour and breadcrumbs. Some garlic. Lots of butter. And the perfect, most magnificent, spectacular chicken you have ever seen.

SERVES 4

- ½ cup (1 stick; 115 g) unsalted butter, softened
- 1 garlic clove, pressed through a garlic press
- 1 tablespoon fresh lemon juice
- 2 teaspoons dried tarragon, divided
- 1 teaspoon dried parsley
- Salt and freshly ground black pepper
- 4 boneless, skinless chicken breast halves (about 6 ounces/170 g each)
- 2 cups (110 g) panko breadcrumbs
- ½ cup (60 g) all-purpose flour
- 2 large eggs, beaten with 2 teaspoons water
- Vegetable oil for frying

In a medium bowl, stir together the butter, garlic, lemon juice, 1 teaspoon of the tarragon, the parsley, ½ teaspoon salt, and ¼ teaspoon pepper; mix well to incorporate the ingredients into the butter. Spread a 12-inch-long (30-cm) piece of plastic wrap or waxed paper on a work surface and mound the butter onto one end, shaping it into a 2-by-3-inch (5-by-7.5-cm) rectangle. Wrap the butter in the plastic and refrigerate for 2 hours or freeze for about 30 minutes.

Rinse and pat dry each chicken breast half and place between two pieces of plastic wrap or waxed paper. Using a meat mallet, pound the breasts evenly to between ¼ and ⅛ inch (3 to 6 mm) thickness. Season each chicken breast lightly with salt and pepper. Cut the chilled butter lengthwise into four equal-size bars and place one in the center of each breast. Fold the ends over the butter and roll up each piece tightly to encase the butter, and roll the breasts into tight logs.

In a shallow dish, whisk together the breadcrumbs, the remaining 1 teaspoon tarragon, 1 teaspoon salt, and ½ teaspoon pepper. Put the flour and eggs into two separate shallow dishes. Dredge each chicken roll in the flour, then the eggs, and, last, the breadcrumbs. Firmly press the breadcrumbs onto the chicken and shake off any excess. Place the chicken in the refrigerator, cover with a clean dish towel, and refrigerate for at least 2 hours or up to overnight.

In a large sauté pan, heat ½ inch (12 mm) of oil over medium-high heat until it registers 375°F (190°C) on a deep-fry thermometer. Add the chicken, seam side down, and reduce the heat to medium-low; cook, turning once, until golden brown and cooked through, about 10 minutes. Using tongs, transfer to a paper towel–lined plate. Serve immediately.

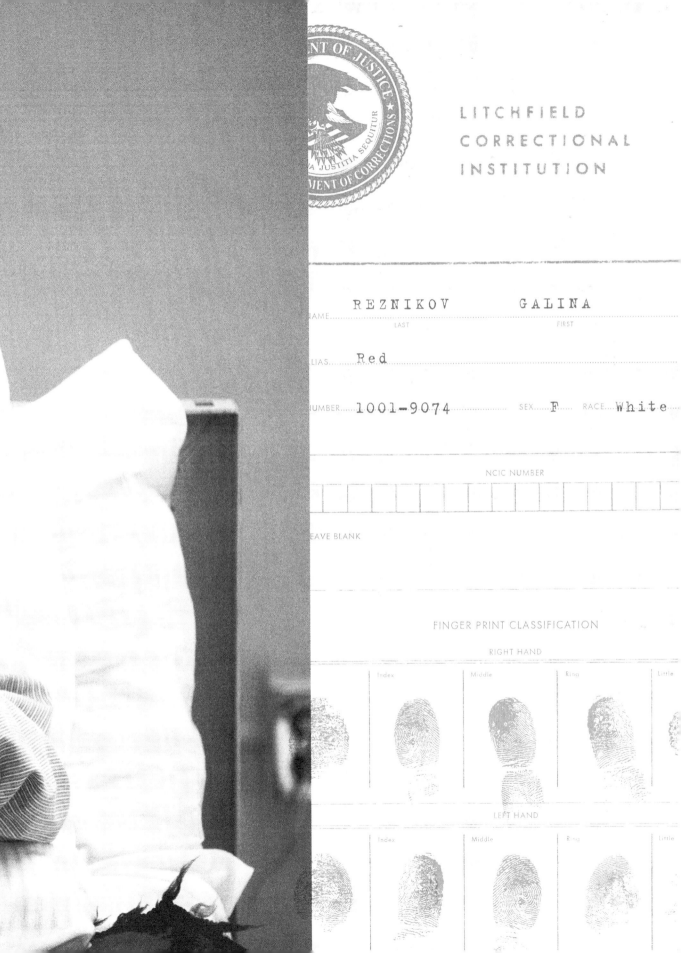

LITCHFIELD
CORRECTIONAL
INSTITUTION

NAME....... **REZNIKOV**   **GALINA**
              LAST   FIRST

ALIAS....... Red

NUMBER.... **1001-9074**............ SEX.....**F**.... RACE....**White**........

NCIC NUMBER

LEAVE BLANK

FINGER PRINT CLASSIFICATION

RIGHT HAND

Index	Middle	Ring	Little

LEFT HAND

Index	Middle	Ring	Little

NUMBER

1006-0878

NAME

MENDOZA, GLORIA

ALIAS

GLORIA'S KITCHEN VS. RED'S KITCHEN

* *

GLORIA'S

Rules:
Don't talk back
You make a mess, you
pick it up
Don't ask me to make you
anything special
No bringing in
any contraband

Favorite Meal:
Easter, it's a big holiday
for us Puerto Ricans.
We used to go to mass
with Mama and come home
for a big feast after.
She always made Arroz con
Gandules. I might try to
make a version of that
this year inside.

Music:
Whatever keeps my girls
from complaining. Flaca
always wants The Smiths.
Girl never shuts up about
some person named "Moz" or
something. Blanca loves
Selena. Always tears up
whenever one of her songs
comes on. Anything from
the 70s that I can dance to
is fine with me. Don't you
dare come in here with
that reggaeton garbage.

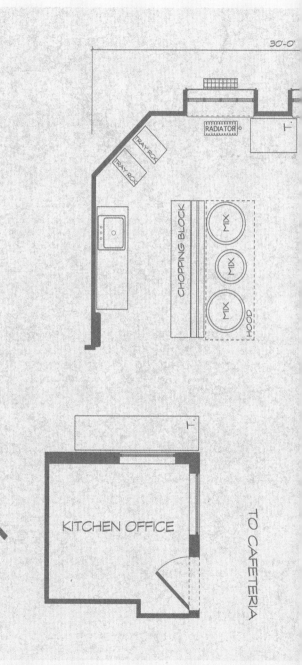

* *

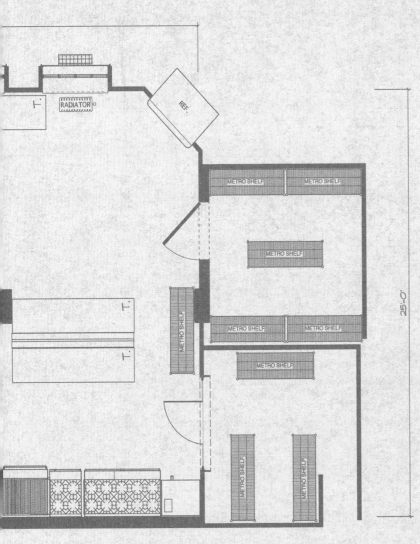

ALIAS   RED

NAME   REZNIKOV, GALINA

NUMBER   1001-9074

RED'S

Rules:
Keep a clean work station
No cross contamination
Always wash your hands
Leave your personal shit back in your bunk

Favorite Meal:
Thanksgiving, being able to cook for everyone and go all out for once, as opposed to working with a federally mandated menu.

Music:
If you're going to have music on in the kitchen, it can't be any of that screeching screaming trash the kids are listening to today. Classical or oldies (50s, 60s, 70s. The 80s and 90s aren't old enough to be called oldies).

HOMEMADE CHINESE FOOD

FOR THE ONE

YOU WANT TO STAY IN WITH

BY POLLY HARPER

Everyone is trying to date today. There's all these dating sites for every single niche of the population. It's exhausting. Luckily I've locked a guy down and he knocked me up, so we're stuck, for better or worse. The best part of having someone by your side till death do you part is ordering in whatever food the monster growing inside of you is craving and scarfing it down on the couch together. No pickles and ice cream for me, I constantly want Chinese food, and not even the authentic stuff. I want greasy, mall-quality, Americanized Chinese food in the classic oyster boxes (if it comes in Styrofoam, you're going to the wrong place). Sometimes Pete insists on a healthier homemade version, "for the sake of the baby." What can you do? Put a couple boxes of chow mein and dumplings in front of me and I'll be passed out in your arms before you know it.

SERVES 2 OR 3

MARINADE

- 1½ teaspoons sherry
- 1 teaspoon peanut oil
- 1½ teaspoons soy sauce
- ¼ teaspoon salt

- 1 pound (455 g) boneless, skinless chicken thighs, cut into ½-inch (12-mm) pieces

SAUCE

- 3 tablespoons fermented chile-bean sauce (see Notes)
- 1 tablespoon rice vinegar
- 2 teaspoons soy sauce
- 2 teaspoons sherry
- 2 teaspoons sugar

COOKING THE CHICKEN

- 1½ tablespoons chicken stock or water
- 2 teaspoons cornstarch
- 2 tablespoons peanut oil

MAKE THE MARINADE:

In a large bowl, whisk together the sherry, oil, soy sauce, and salt. Add the chicken and stir to coat it with the marinade. Cover and set aside for 30 minutes at room temperature or in the refrigerator for up to 4 hours.

MAKE THE SAUCE:

In a small bowl, whisk together the chile-bean sauce, vinegar, soy sauce, sherry, and sugar.

COOK THE CHICKEN:

In a small bowl, whisk together the stock and cornstarch to create a slurry. Set aside.

Heat the oil in a large skillet or wok over medium-high heat. Add the Sichuan peppercorns, chiles, scallion whites, garlic, and ginger and cook for about 1 minute, until aromatic and the garlic and ginger are lightly browned. Add the chicken in one layer and cook without moving it for 2 minutes, then continue to cook, stirring often, until cooked through and lightly browned, about 5 minutes. Add the sauce and bring to a boil; cook for 2 minutes, then add the cornstarch slurry and cook until thickened and slightly glossy, about 30 seconds. Transfer to a serving bowl, top with the scallion greens and peanuts, and serve immediately.

- 2 to 3 teaspoons Sichuan peppercorns (see Notes), to taste

- 3 dried red chiles, seeds removed or not

- 2 scallions, whites minced and greens thinly sliced (reserved separately)

- 2 garlic cloves, minced

- 2 teaspoons minced fresh ginger

- ⅓ cup (50 g) roasted unsalted peanuts

NOTES: Chile-bean sauce is a spicy reddish-brown sauce made from fermented soybeans and chiles. You can find jars of it at Asian markets.

The Sichuan peppercorn, not actually a peppercorn but a reddish brown berry that comes from the prickly ash tree, is a key ingredient in Sichuan cooking. Its signature characteristic is the tingling, numbing (and addictive) sensation it causes in the mouth, which allows you to tolerate the hot chiles that are often served in dishes that feature it. Use only the open reddish pods, not the black seeds, which are bitter in taste and gritty in texture. If your peppercorns come closed, lightly crush them and remove any seeds; remove any twigs scattered among the peppercorns as well.

PETE'S
PINEAPPLE-MARINATED
"CARIBOU"
WITH PINEAPPLE SALSA

BY PETE HARPER

There's nothing like killing an animal with your bare hands, cooking and consuming it, absorbing its energy and knowledge. And by bare hands, I mean the guide you've hired and his high-powered rifle, with you right next to him. Now, some may feel you should fast on a vision quest, but not me. I say take in as much of Mother Nature as you can. Walking across the frozen tundra of Alaska really works up an appetite. It's not like I was snacking on trail mix and beef jerky (unless things got really dodgy). The best thing to do is find your spirit animal in the wilderness, line him up in your sights, and take the beast down. A day-long hunt will make you good and knackered, so make sure your cabin is nearby.

SERVES 2

MARINADE

- **½ cup (120 ml) fresh or bottled pineapple juice**
- **2 tablespoons fresh lemon juice**
- **3 tablespoons soy sauce**
- **3 tablespoons brown sugar**
- **1 tablespoon olive oil**
- **1 teaspoon ground ginger**
- **½ teaspoon dry mustard powder**
- **1 teaspoon salt**
- **3 garlic cloves, pressed through a garlic press**
- **1 tablespoon Tabasco sauce**
- **Two 10- to 12-ounce (280- to 340-g) caribou, venison, or beef steaks (about 1½ inches/4 centimeters thick), trimmed of visible fat**

MARINATE THE STEAKS:

In a medium bowl, whisk together all the marinade ingredients until the sugar dissolves. Place the meat in a zip-top bag, add the marinade, seal the bag, and massage the marinade all over the meat. Refrigerate for 24 to 48 hours.

MAKE THE SALSA:

In a large bowl, combine the pineapple, onion, bell pepper, jalapeño, and mint. In a small bowl, whisk together the lime juice and salt. Add the lime juice mixture to the pineapple mixture and toss to coat.

COOK THE STEAKS:

Remove the meat from the marinade. Set up an open-fire grill and cook till desired doneness, the rarer the better for most tender results, especially if you are using caribou or venison, which are very lean.

If the great outdoors isn't an option, heat a cast-iron pan over medium-high heat for 5 minutes. Add a touch of oil, place the steaks in the pan, and resist touching them for 4 minutes to create

SALSA

- 1 cup (180 g) finely chopped fresh pineapple (see Note)
- 1 tablespoon finely chopped red onion
- ½ small red bell pepper, finely chopped
- 1 small jalapeño chile, seeds removed or kept in for more heat, finely chopped
- 1 tablespoon finely chopped fresh mint
- 1½ tablespoons fresh lime juice, or to taste
- ¼ teaspoon salt, or to taste

- Peanut oil, if cooking in a pan
- 2 tablespoons unsalted butter, if cooking in a pan

a nice crust, then flip them and add the butter. Cook for 3 to 4 minutes, basting with the butter, until rare to medium-rare. Place the steaks on a cutting board, let rest for 5 minutes, and serve with the salsa alongside.

NOTE: For enhanced flavor, throw the pineapple on the grill to char it before chopping.

GINA MURPHY   LORNA MORELLO   TIFFANY JEFFERSON

BEST INMATE JOBS - ACCORDING TO THE INMATES

****

Warehouse Clerk
* Highest pay in the prison camp, up to 75 cents an hour!
* Ideal for skimming incoming materials from the trucks.
* Good source of contraband as the point of entry between the prison and the outside world.
* Basic math is required.

Librarian
* Most privacy of any job for an inmate, as most COs hate books and education.
* Best access to information and legal books which gives you a leg up when it comes to appeals, prison disciplinary hearings, and pardon-letter writing.
* Good place to hook up.
* Literacy required.

Assistant Food Service Manager
* Best access to food and food-related contraband.
* Better to be an assistant to the manager. The buck does not stop with you when it comes to the stress of feeding every inmate three times a day, seven days a week. You just got to be supportive.

Van Driver
* Allows for freedom of movement within the camp as well as access to the outside world.
* Greater contact with COs allows van drivers to have accurate knowledge and information of prison operations and gossip among the staff.
* Van drivers are required to pass a driver's test and have a strong understanding of mechanical and automotive repair.

Visitation Room Photographer
* Framing photos for inmates with their loved ones is one of the few creative outlets in prison that also pays a wage.
* The photographer must tidy up the visitation room before and especially after the visitors have left. It can get messy.
* Requires a short training session on uploading photos to computers.

TIFFANY DOGGETT   DAYANARA DIAZ   JANAE WATSON

WORST INMATE JOBS - ACCORDING TO THE INMATES

* *

Cleaning Orderly

* Orderlies are expected to clean staff areas, which are carefully inspected by COs. Failure to get a floor spotless can land you in trouble.
* This job is measured by quota (number of toilets cleaned) rather than by the hour. An ambitious inmate might clear 80 cents of toilets in an hour. However, unambitious inmates are usually assigned to the cleaning crew.

Grounds Crew

* If you don't mind bugs, poison ivy, and the occasional snake, this job would be great April through September. But the rest of the year it's freezing.

* Grounds crew includes physical labor such as removing fallen branches after storms or shoveling snow in the winter, which are very strenuous.

Laundry Supervisor

* The smells in laundry get horrific, both from the dirty clothes but also from the chemicals used in the washers.
* There is also an odorless gas that all inmates know is coming from the tubes connecting the dryers to the ventilation grates.

Recreation Activities Planner

* You are at the center of the biggest arguments in the camp: which holidays

get color posters instead of black and white, and what movie to watch each week.
* The upside is that sometimes the rec planner leaves camp to decorate a men's prison. If you like that sort of thing, have at it.

Maintenance Assistant

* This job isn't so bad if you know a thing or two about electrical currents and leach lines. Otherwise you will get yourself electrocuted.
* The supervisor is usually an actual plumber who can be a suffocating jerk about security since your tool belt includes screwdrivers and other dangerous objects.

PIROZHKI

(RUSSIAN MEAT STUFFED BUNS)

BY GALINA "RED" REZNIKOV

Smell is powerful. A moment of inhaling the steamy, sweet warmth of a pirozhok, and I have the most vivid memories: Picking mushrooms with my papa at our dacha, he would bring along snacks to keep us going all day. The sounds of an accordion and guitar, played by a summer campfire while my classmates and I drank to our youth and ate pirozhki to keep us going till dawn. The first lonely year in America when all I wanted to do was turn back and go home, I would bake a batch of pirozhki, drink to my motherland, and find the strength to go forward.

MAKES ABOUT 40

PASTRY

- 3¼ cups (400 g) all-purpose flour
- 1 teaspoon baking powder
- ¼ teaspoon salt
- ½ cup (1 stick; 115 g) unsalted butter, chilled and cut into small pieces
- 2 large eggs
- 1 cup (240 ml) sour cream

FILLING

- 2 tablespoons olive oil
- 1 onion, finely chopped
- 2 garlic cloves, minced
- 1 tablespoon dill seeds
- 1 pound (455 g) ground beef
- 2 cups (7 ounces/200 g) finely chopped cabbage (from about ¼ medium head)
- 4 scallions, finely chopped
- 1 teaspoon balsamic vinegar
- Salt and freshly ground black pepper

- 1 large egg yolk, lightly beaten
- 1 teaspoon heavy cream

MAKE THE PASTRY:

Put the flour, baking powder, and salt in a food processor and pulse a few times to combine. Add the butter, eggs, and sour cream and process until thoroughly blended and a loose dough is formed, about 30 seconds. Dump the mixture out onto a lightly floured work surface and give it a very light knead, just until a smooth dough is formed. Form the dough into 2 balls, press the balls into disks, and wrap each disk in plastic wrap. Refrigerate for at least 2 hours (you can prepare the dough up to 2 days in advance).

MAKE THE FILLING:

In a large skillet, heat the oil over medium heat. Add the onion and cook, stirring occasionally, until softened, about 5 minutes. Add the garlic and cook for 1 minute. Add the dill seeds and beef and cook, stirring to break up any lumps in the meat, until the meat is starting to brown and there are no pink spots remaining, about 10 minutes. Add the cabbage and scallions and cook, stirring, until completely wilted, about 5 minutes. Add the vinegar and season with salt and pepper. Transfer the filling to a large bowl and set aside to cool (or spread it out over a baking sheet for quicker cooling action).

ROLL OUT THE DOUGH:

On a lightly floured work surface using a floured rolling pin, roll out the pastry ⅛ inch (3 mm) thick. Using a 3-inch (7.5-cm) round cookie cutter, cut the dough into rounds and discard the scraps.

The dough may shrink a little after cutting; after all the rounds have been cut out, roll each with the rolling pin to flatten them so they measure between 3½ and 4 inches (9 and 10 cm). In a small bowl, beat the egg yolk together with the cream. Brush each pastry round with the egg wash.

FILL AND BAKE THE BUNS:

Preheat the oven to 400°F (200°C). Line two baking sheets with parchment paper or silicone mats.

Using about 1 tablespoon of filling for each circle of dough, shape the filling into an oval and place it on the half of the circle of dough closest to you. Fold the other half of the circle of dough over to enclose the filling. Press the edges of the dough with your fingers or the tines of a fork to seal. Brush the tops with egg wash. (If there is any leftover filling, you could serve it over rice for a bonus meal.) Arrange the buns on the prepared baking sheets, place in the oven, and bake for about 15 minutes, until browned on top. Let cool slightly and serve.

VEGETARIAN STUFFED RED PEPPERS (a Neptune's Produce Special)

BY .... GALINA "RED" REZNIKOV

There is something really wrong with vegetarians. They are silly, bourgeois, and most important, they don't eat meat. But don't tell that to my grandkids. The oldest saw the Bambi movie and he convinced all the others any meat they ate was a cartoon they loved. And my weak-willed son wouldn't stand up to them. That's how Dmitri and I found ourselves learning to cook vegetarian food. We started with meatless salads, then we moved on to stuffed peppers. For our grandkids' sake, we took time and care, preparing each pepper and arranging them into a colorful presentation. It was a huge hit, and the adults were lining up for them in no time. Now, even in here, the meat lovers are envious and we make a double batch.

MAKES .... 8 STUFFED PEPPERS

INGREDIENTS

8 bell peppers, any color

Salt

½ ounce (15 g) dried porcini mushrooms

3 tablespoons extra-virgin olive oil

1 onion, finely chopped

3 garlic cloves, minced

1½ pounds (680 g) white mushrooms, finely chopped

Freshly ground black pepper

2 teaspoons dried thyme

2 tablespoons white wine

One 14.5-ounce (411-g) can diced tomatoes

2 tablespoons finely chopped fresh parsley, plus more for topping

(continued)

INSTRUCTIONS

Line a large plate with paper towels. Cut the stem end from the bell peppers ½ inch (12 mm) from the top and remove the cores and seeds. Finely chop the flesh from around the stem and set aside to use for the filling.

Place a large pot of water over high heat and bring to a boil; generously season with salt. Add the peppers and press down on them with tongs to submerge the cavities in the water. Cook until the peppers just begin to soften, about 3 minutes. Using tongs, remove the peppers, drain the water from the insides, then place the peppers cut side up on the prepared plate.

Position an oven rack in the middle of the oven and preheat the oven to 350°F (175°C).

In a small bowl, soak the dried porcini mushrooms in ⅔ cup (150 ml) warm water for about 15 minutes, until softened. Remove the mushrooms and strain the soaking liquid through a coffee filter or small strainer lined with a dampened paper towel; reserve the mushroom soaking liquid and finely chop the mushrooms.

INGREDIENTS

3 cups (560 g) cooked medium-grain white rice

8 ounces (225 g) Monterey Jack cheese, shredded (about 2 cups)

INSTRUCTIONS

Heat the oil in a large skillet over medium heat. Add the onion and reserved chopped bell pepper and cook until softened, about 5 minutes. Add the garlic and cook for 1 minute. Add the fresh mushrooms, season with salt and lots of pepper, and cook until softened, about 10 minutes. Add the soaked dried mushrooms and thyme and cook for 2 minutes. Add the reserved mushroom soaking liquid and the wine and stir until mostly evaporated, about 1 minute. Add the tomatoes and cook for about 5 minutes, until most of the liquid in the pan is absorbed. Stir in the parsley and remove from the heat.

Transfer the mushroom mixture to a large bowl, add the rice, then add 1½ cups (165 g) of the cheese. Taste and adjust the seasonings.

Divide the mushroom mixture among the peppers, filling them a little over the brim, and place them in a 9-by-13-inch (23-by-33-cm) baking dish, propping them up one against the next so they stay upright in the pan. Top with the remaining ½ cup (55 g) grated cheese. Bake until the cheese is browned and bubbly and the filling is heated through, 25 to 30 minutes. Sprinkle with parsley and serve immediately.

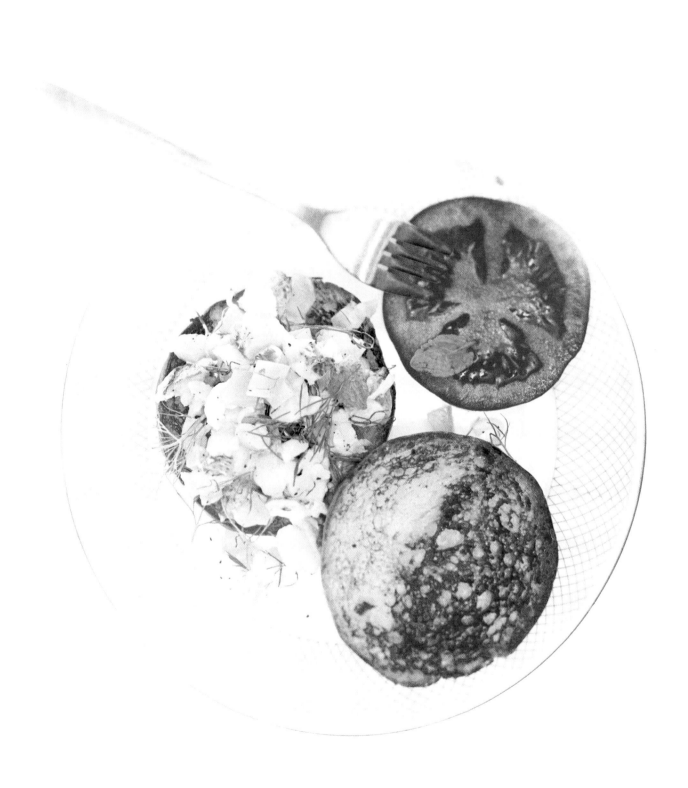

LOBSTER SLIDERS

BY NATALIE "FIG" FIGUEROA

I deal with a bunch of imbeciles all day, so when I get to step outside Litchfield's doors and throw a function, I vet the caterers within an inch of their lives. If there are going to be people representing me in front of campaign contributors—er, I mean guests—you bet your ass they're going to be the best money can buy. I would love to be able to make all of this food for everyone, but who has the time when they run a federal prison 24/7/365? The food is from old Figueroa family recipes. I make sure all of the food we serve at events comes from family recipes, because America was founded on tradition. Without the past, we'll be left with nothing for the future. And that's why even the smallest donation would be so appreciated, so we can secure the safety of our children's futures. Slider?

MAKES 8 SLIDERS

- 8 ounces (225 g) cooked lobster meat (about 1¼ cups), cut into ¼-inch (.5-cm) pieces (from one 1½- to 2-pound/680- to 910-g cooked lobster)
- 3 tablespoons mayonnaise
- ¼ cup (30 g) minced fennel bulb
- 1 tablespoon minced fresh fennel fronds
- 1 tablespoon finely minced preserved lemon
- Squeeze of lemon juice, plus more if needed
- Salt and coarsely ground black pepper
- 2 tablespoons unsalted butter, softened
- Eight mini brioche rolls, split
- 1 large plum tomato, cut into 8 thin slices
- Handful of fresh mint leaves

In a medium bowl, combine the lobster with the mayonnaise, fennel bulb, fennel fronds, preserved lemon, and lemon juice. Taste and season with salt if needed and give it a generous grind of the peppermill and a little more lemon juice if needed.

Lightly butter the cut side of each roll. Heat a large skillet over medium-high heat. Toast the rolls in the skillet, cut side down, until lightly browned, about 1 minute. Transfer the rolls to a platter. Spoon some of the lobster mixture on the bottom half of each roll. Top with a tomato slice and some mint leaves. Close the sliders and serve.

NACKS

004

& SIDES

FOR SURVIVAL

CHERRY CHOCOLATE KISS SMOOTHIE

BY LARRY BLOOM

Pipes used to set out the ingredients for my smoothie every morning. If you or someone close to you doesn't like to eat fruit, do them a favor and make them a fruit smoothie. Get your daily fruit intake! What flavor is the best? Papaya and orange, peach with mango, I even like a good peanut butter and apple smoothie (it's better than you'd think!). But cherry smoothies are my favorite. They taste good. They're healthy. And most importantly, they're sexy. Cherries are the perfect fruit for hot phone sex talk. Say "tight," "little," and "cherry" enough, add in a load of heavy breathing, and you'll have her begging for your banana, which is hopefully her favorite fruit.

SERVES 1

- ½ cup (70 g) pitted fresh or frozen sweet cherries
- 1 frozen sliced banana
- ¾ cup (180 ml) dairy milk or unsweetened almond or soy milk, plus more as needed
- ¼ cup (60 ml) pure cherry juice, plus more as needed
- 3 tablespoons cacao powder
- ¼ teaspoon almond extract
- Pinch of salt
- 1 teaspoon cacao nibs (optional)

In a blender, combine all the ingredients except the cacao nibs and blend until smooth; add a little more milk or cherry juice if the smoothie is too thick. Pour into a glass, top with the cacao nibs, if using, and serve.

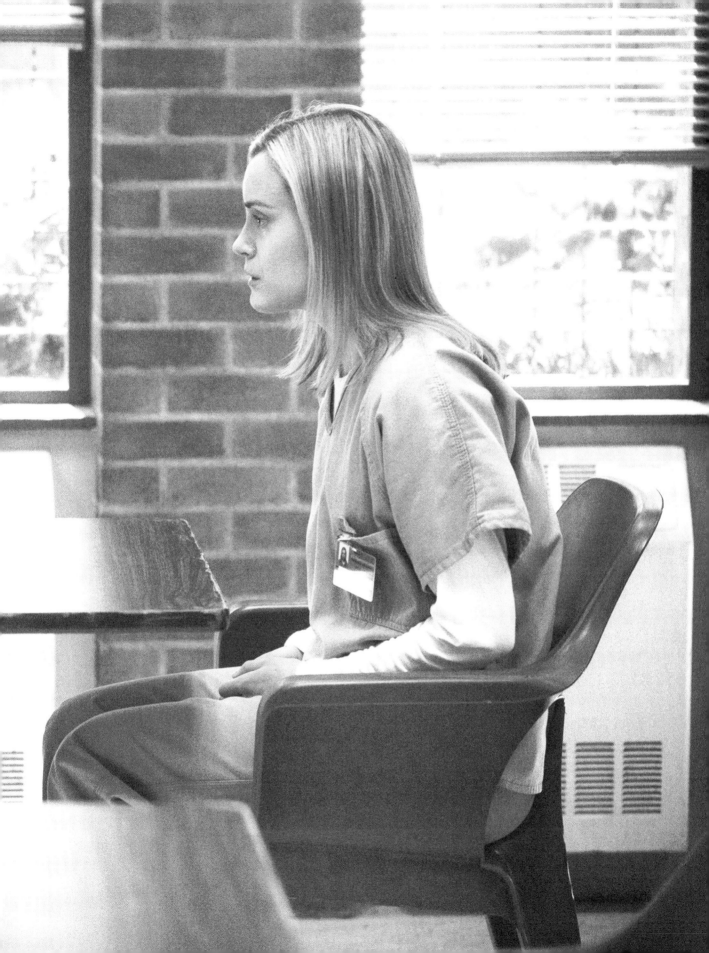

CRACK ALMONDS

BY PIPER CHAPMAN

You don't really know how much you'll miss something until it's gone. My trips to the farmers' market, shopping at Whole Foods, and having a fully stocked pantry: That's what I miss. When it came to shopping, Larry was hopeless when we first started dating. I think his mother shopped for him until we moved in together. I taught him the basics, but he's always had a good eye for snacks. He found these "crack almonds," as we came to call them. God, they're dangerous to have around. Before you know it, you've eaten a whole bag of them and you're filled with deliciousness and regret. They're covered in brown sugar, so they leave a little granule trail wherever you go. I'd make Larry hide them from me, but he's so bad at hiding things I would always find them. He'd know because I'd be caught red-handed with brown sugar all over my face. A criminal in my own home.

MAKES ABOUT 1 CUP (160 G)
—make in small batches because of their addictive nature

- 1 cup (140 g) almonds, roughly chopped
- 3 tablespoons dark brown sugar
- ¼ teaspoon salt

Line a baking sheet with parchment paper.

Preheat a medium cast-iron skillet over medium heat. Add the almonds and toast, stirring often, for 3 to 5 minutes, until lightly browned. Sprinkle the brown sugar and salt over the almonds and cook, stirring almost continuously with a wooden spoon, until the brown sugar is completely melted and darkened in color, watching the skillet carefully so the almonds don't burn, 3 to 5 minutes. Spread the almonds in a single layer on the prepared baking sheet and let cool completely, then break up any clumps with your hands and get to work on eating your fill.

CHANG'S STICKY-FINGERS MOVIE NIGHT POPCORN BALLS

BY .... **MEI CHANG**

My father told me many times, "You want to make a lotta money, you gotta be strong like hard metal. The customer always want a better price. But you must not listen to the excuses." Same in prison. Nobody want popcorn all week. Girls want candy. Or chips. But no popcorn. Not me. I plan ahead for the future and take all the popcorn. Then on movie night, every girl come to me and say, "You got some butter popcorn?" I give fair price if they come early. But the closer to movie time, the more the price. Some girls tell me sad story, "I lost my stamps. I didn't remember it was movie night." I say, "Fuck off, bitch." In the end, they always pay.

MAKES .... **ABOUT 36**

INGREDIENTS

- 8 cups (100 g) popped popcorn (from about ⅓ cup/70 g kernels)

- ½ cup (1 stick; 115 g) unsalted butter, plus more for buttering your hands

- ½ cup (120 ml) honey

- ½ teaspoon salt

- 1 teaspoon vanilla extract

INSTRUCTIONS

Preheat the oven to 325°F (160°C). Spread the popcorn out over a baking sheet in a single layer. Line a separate baking sheet with waxed paper or parchment paper.

In a medium saucepan, combine the butter, honey, and salt. Place over medium heat and using a heat-proof spatula or wooden spoon, stir until the butter is melted. Increase the heat to medium-high, bring to a boil, and boil, stirring constantly, for 1 minute. Remove from the heat and stir in the vanilla.

Slowly pour the butter mixture over the popcorn and stir gently to coat completely. Bake the popcorn, stirring every 5 minutes, until the liquid is just starting to dry (you don't want the popcorn to get overly crisp or it won't form into a ball), about 25 minutes. Remove from the oven and let the popcorn stand for about 5 minutes, until just cool enough to handle. Lightly butter your hands and quickly press small handfuls of the mixture into 1½-inch (4-cm) balls, loosening any popcorn that sticks to the bottom of pan with a spatula as you work. If the popcorn mixture cools too much to be malleable, return it to the oven for about a minute to soften.

INGREDIENTS

INSTRUCTIONS

As you make the popcorn balls, put them on the prepared baking sheet and let cool completely. Store in an airtight container, where they will keep for up to 2 weeks.

VARIATIONS

MOLASSES POPCORN BALLS: Cook 1 tablespoon molasses and $\frac{1}{2}$ teaspoon ground cinnamon with the butter and honey mixture.

NO BALLS POPCORN: Make the popcorn as directed above, with or without the molasses option; leave it in the oven for an extra 5 minutes, until it starts to get crisp. Remove from the oven and let cool completely. Break the popcorn up with a spatula, scraping the pan to get at all of it. Bag it, and pop in a movie.

LITCHFIELD
CORRECTIONAL
INSTITUTION

NAME...... **JEFFERSON** .... **TASHA** ....
                      LAST   FIRST

ALIAS...... **Taystee** ....

NUMBER...... **1165-1902** .... SEX.... **F** .... RACE...... **Black**

NCIC NUMBER

LEAVE BLANK

FINGER PRINT CLASSIFICATION

RIGHT HAND

Thumb	Index	Middle	Ring	Little

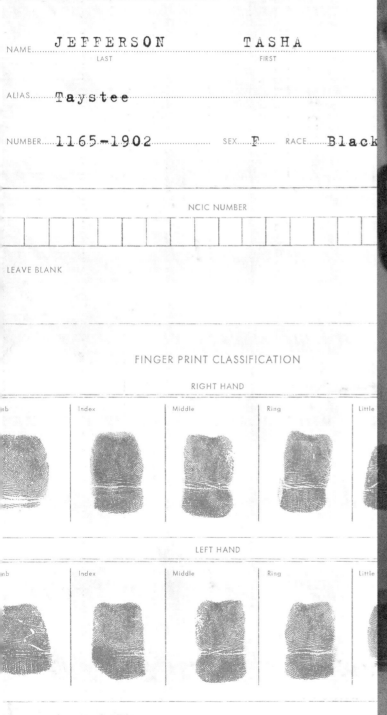

LEFT HAND

Thumb	Index	Middle	Ring	Little

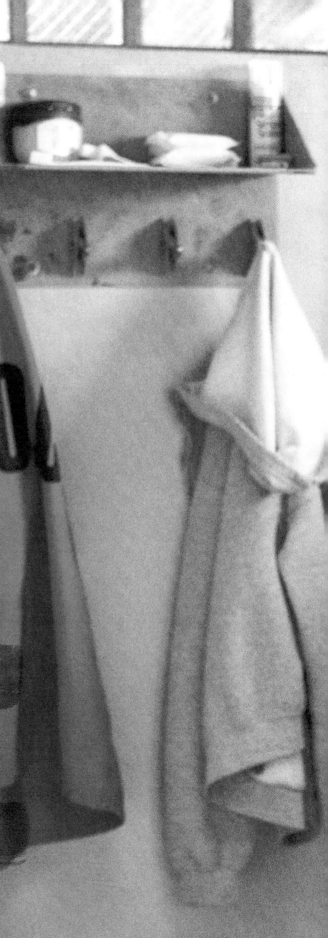

TAYSTEE'S THAILAND ROOSTER HOT SAUCE

BY ...... TASHA "TAYSTEE" JEFFERSON

Only thing worse than being in prison is being in prison without the Rooster Sauce. Outside they put it on everything: chicken wings, potato chips, jerky, pizza. I bet they even make Thai hot sauce ice cream in some fancy place in California or wherever they got a lot of Thais at. If you wanna get really fancy and impress someone with your skills, make your own sauce. We made ours in here all the time till Healy hooked me up. It didn't take away the fences, and it didn't take away the noise, but it sure gave the Good N' Plenty a nice kick.

MAKES ...... ABOUT 1 CUP (240 ML)

INGREDIENTS

1½ pounds (680 g) serrano, Fresno, or red jalapeño chiles (or a mixture), stems removed but green tops left on, cut in half (see Note)

6 garlic cloves, peeled

5 tablespoons dark brown sugar or palm sugar

2 teaspoons salt

½ cup (120 ml) distilled white vinegar

(continued)

INSTRUCTIONS

In a food processor, combine the chiles, garlic, sugar, and salt and pulse until the mixture forms a coarse paste, stopping the machine and scraping the sides of the bowl once or twice as needed. Transfer the mixture to a glass jar and press down on the solids with a meat mallet, large pestle, or similar implement until a briny liquid rises and covers the surface of the chiles. Cover loosely, place the jar on a rimmed plate to catch any potential bubbling over, and let sit in a cool place out of direct sunlight to ferment, opening the lid and stirring each day, then pressing on the solids to keep the mixture covered in brine, until the mixture no longer rises in volume from the action of the fermentation, 3 to 5 days total. (The mixture will start to ferment in 1 to 2 days; you'll know it's fermenting when you start to see bubbles at the bottom of the jar.)

Transfer the chiles to a blender, add the vinegar, and blend until completely smooth, 2 to 3 minutes. Place a fine-mesh strainer over a medium saucepan and strain the chiles into the saucepan, using a

INGREDIENTS

INSTRUCTIONS

rubber spatula or wooden spoon to press down and extract as much sauce as possible. Discard the seeds remaining in the strainer or save them to flavor soups, stews, and the like. Place the saucepan over medium-high heat, bring to a boil, then reduce the heat to medium and cook at a high simmer until the sauce thickens, 10 to 15 minutes. Taste and adjust the flavors with more sugar, salt, or vinegar if needed. Cool completely, then transfer to a squeeze bottle and store in the refrigerator, where it will keep for up to 6 months.

NOTE:

When you are blending the chiles, the fumes are quite strong and can bring on a coughing fit. Protect yourself by making sure you are working in a well-ventilated area and cover the food processor and blender with a kitchen towel to keep the fumes from escaping.

GLORIA'S RICE AND BEANS

BY .... GLORIA MENDOZA

Cooking is the best way to keep your man. My mom always said that. These days, at least my cooking keeps the mouths at dinner full and quiet. But you know what? My mom was right about men. You think a big ass is enough? No. My mom's ass was bigger than mine, and my dad was gone before I was born. Now, don't get me wrong. You gotta be a strong woman. You gotta stand up for yourself, for your kids. But if you know how to cook some good arroz con habichuelas, your man will do anything you say. Except clear his own place. But that's what kids are for.

SERVES 4

INGREDIENTS

2 tablespoons olive oil

1 large onion, finely chopped

1 large green bell pepper, cored, seeded, and finely chopped

3 garlic cloves, minced

1 teaspoon ground cumin

¼ to ½ teaspoon ground cayenne, to taste

1 tablespoon rum

One 14.5-ounce (411-g) can diced tomatoes

3 cups (530 g) cooked black or red beans or a combination (two 15-ounce/425-g cans), drained

Salt

½ cup (50 g) pitted green olives, roughly chopped (optional)

½ cup (15 g) roughly chopped fresh cilantro

4 cups (630 g) warm cooked long-grain white rice

INSTRUCTIONS

Heat the oil in a large saucepan over medium heat. Add the onion and bell pepper and sauté for about 5 minutes, until softened. Add the garlic and cook for 2 minutes, or until softened. Add the cumin and cayenne and cook, stirring, until aromatic, about 1 minute. Add the rum and cook, stirring to release any stuck bits from the bottom of the pan, for 1 minute. Add the tomatoes, bring to a simmer, cover, and cook, stirring occasionally, for 5 minutes. Stir in the beans, season with salt, cover, and cook for 20 minutes, stirring occasionally, to blend the flavors; add a little water if the mixture starts to get dry or the beans stick to the bottom of the pan. Stir in the olives, if using, then stir in the cilantro, taste, and add more salt if needed. Serve over the rice.

LITCHFIELD
CORRECTIONAL
INSTITUTION

NAME	BLACK	CARRIE
	LAST	FIRST

ALIAS.... Big Boo

NUMBER.... 1965-1010   SEX.... F   RACE.... White

NCIC NUMBER

LEAVE BLANK

FINGER PRINT CLASSIFICATION

RIGHT HAND

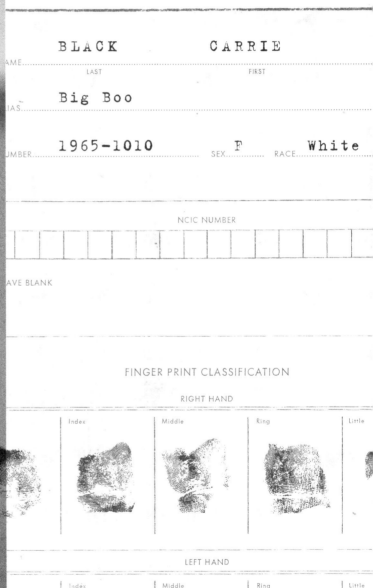

| Index | Middle | Ring | Little |

LEFT HAND

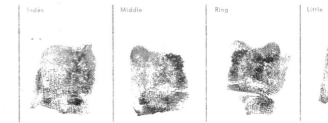

| Index | Middle | Ring | Little |

BIG BOO'S ROASTED CORN

BY CARRIE "BIG BOO" BLACK

A little advice for the playas out there: High-society ladies, poor little country girls, even foreigners with BO, they all love a big, yellow, buttered cob of corn. Will they get their fingers dirty? Yes. Will it get stuck in their teeth? Yes. But even if that salty yumminess runs down their faces, they will love every kernel of it. Oh yes they will. Now, some of you out there might be saying, "Hold on there. What do you know about foreigners?" I know plenty. I haven't spent my whole life locked up. I've traveled the world. I've crossed the great ocean. Did you know they even eat grilled corn in Cambodia? The corn is just much smaller. And you know what that means: I can fit more in my mouth.

SERVES 1

INGREDIENTS

1 ear of corn, husked, silks removed

1 lime wedge

1/8 teaspoon salt

Large pinch of chile powder

INSTRUCTIONS

Turn a gas burner to medium (see Note). Place the corn directly over the burner and cook, turning with the corn's handle every couple minutes, until blackened all over, about 10 minutes.

Meanwhile, squeeze the lime onto a plate. Add the salt and chile powder; place the squeezed lime half directly onto the mixture and work the ingredients together. Use the lime wedge to smear the corn with the seasoned lime juice. Eat immediately.

NOTE:

If you don't have a burner, you can roast your corn in the oven by placing it on a roasting pan and broiling in a preheated broiler for about 10 minutes, turning frequently, until blackened all over. This is a good way to make multiple ears of blackened corn.

SHU THANKSGIVING STUFFING LOAF

BY .... ANONYMOUS

I've been in here for three weeks, I think. I can't really tell anymore. There's no clock and the lights are always on in SHU. My eyes used to water when I tried to go to sleep, thanks to these fluorescent bulbs, but they've been bone dry for at least the past few hours . . . days? I try and keep track of the time by when meals are delivered, if you can even call them that. Figuring out what day it is is the only way to stomach what comes on that tray. I think there's a holiday coming up. Veterans Day? Arbor Day? Holidays used to mean home-cooked meals and arguing with my sister about getting handsy with my boyfriend at the dinner table. Now it just means reading the same goddamn book over and over and eating the rejects from that Kitchen Horror Stories show.

SERVES .... 10 TO 12 AS A SIDE DISH

INGREDIENTS

One 1-pound (455-g) loaf French or Italian bread

½ cup (1 stick; 115 g) unsalted butter

1 large onion, chopped

2 celery ribs, chopped

2 large Granny Smith apples, peeled, cored, and chopped

¼ cup (15 g) chopped fresh sage, or 4 teaspoons dried sage

½ teaspoon freshly ground black pepper

2 cups (480 ml) vegetable or chicken stock

3 large eggs, lightly beaten

1 teaspoon salt

INSTRUCTIONS

Preheat the oven to 300°F (150°C). Butter a 9-by-13-inch (23-by-33-cm) baking dish.

Trim the crusty ends from the bread and using a serrated knife, cut it into slices ½ inch (12 mm) thick. Cut the slices crosswise into ½-inch (12-mm) cubes. Arrange the cubes in two baking pans in a single layer. Place the pans in the oven and bake for 10 to 15 minutes, stirring once or twice, until golden and crisp. Remove from the oven and set aside to cool.

Increase the oven temperature to 400°F (200°C). Melt the butter in a large skillet over medium heat. Pour 2 tablespoons of the butter into a small bowl and set aside. Add the onion, celery, and apples to the skillet and sauté, stirring occasionally, until softened, about 15 minutes. Stir in the sage and pepper and cook until aromatic, about 1 minute. Transfer the mixture to a large bowl and add the bread cubes.

In a medium bowl, whisk the stock into the eggs and add the salt. Add to the bread cube mixture and toss gently to coat the dry ingredients. Place the mixture into the prepared baking dish, drizzle with the reserved melted butter, cover tightly with foil, and bake for 20 minutes, then remove the foil and bake until the top is golden brown and crusty, 15 to 20 minutes longer.

LITCHFIELD CORRECTIONAL INSTITUTION / LITCHFIELD, NEW YORK

"Just a little something extra for the holidays."

NAME
—GEORGE "PORNSTACHE" MENDEZ

RED'S THANKSGIVING GRAVY (without the drippings)

GALINA "RED" REZNIKOV

BY . . . .

Thanksgiving is a pretty foreign concept to a Russian. I couldn't wrap my head around it when we emigrated from the motherland to America. The fourth Thursday in November everyone gathers to gorge themselves on turkey — a protein that's not worth a damn. We joined with a few other Russian families on our block, embracing a holiday we didn't understand the meaning of. I was in charge of bringing coyc, the gravy, something I'm quite familiar with. When we all sat at the dinner table, confronted with this foreign meal, nobody spoke. Finally, Dmitri broke the ice by grabbing the turkey's leg, exclaiming, "Let's feast!" Looking around, I watched these families that were just like us. Strangers in a strange land. We were pilgrims in our own right, making a better life in the New World. I'll never forget that first Thanksgiving and because of it, Thanksgiving is my favorite holiday, even in this place.

MAKES . . . . . ABOUT 3 CUPS (700 ML) . . . .

INGREDIENTS	INSTRUCTIONS
4 tablespoons (½ stick; 55 g) unsalted butter	In a medium saucepan, melt the butter over medium-high heat. Whisk in the flour and cook, stirring frequently, for about 2 minutes, until a golden blond roux is formed.
¼ cup (30 g) all-purpose flour	
4 cups (1 L) turkey stock	
2 tablespoons dry sherry	Slowly whisk in the stock, making sure to break up any lumps, bring to a boil, then reduce the heat and simmer until reduced by about one quarter and the mixture is thickened but still pourable, about 15 minutes. Stir in the sherry, cream, and herbs and cook for 1 minute to warm through. Remove from the heat and season with salt and pepper. Serve immediately or let cool, transfer to a container, cover, and store in the refrigerator for up to 1 week. Reheat just before serving.
2 tablespoons heavy cream	
1 tablespoon finely minced fresh sage, thyme, or rosemary, or a combination	
Salt and freshly ground black pepper	

TAYSTEE'S
SWEET & HOT CHICKEN WINGS

BY TASHA "TAYSTEE" JEFFERSON

There are many tales as to how the almighty chicken wing came to be. Some say it was an on-the-spot bar snack creation, others say it was created out of necessity after a bar's owner was trapped inside during a blizzard with nothing more than chicken scraps. I say it's tasty as hell so I don't really care where it comes from. They're the perfect size, they get you nice and messy while you eat, and they pack a punch. All they got in this prison is bland-ass food, and it makes me crave the heat of a good plate of wings more than anything. I hope that chicken shows up again in the yard so I can satisfy this craving.

SERVES 4 AS A STARTER OR SNACK

- **Vegetable oil for frying**

- **3 tablespoons Rooster Sauce, homemade (page 119) or store-bought**

- **2 tablespoons rice vinegar**

- **¼ cup (60 ml) honey**

- **2 pounds (910 g) chicken wings, separated at the joint**

- **¼ cup (30 g) cornstarch**

- **Salt**

- **3 tablespoons unsalted butter, cut into pieces**

- **2 scallions, white and green parts, thinly sliced**

- **Sour cream (optional)**

In a large pot, heat 2 inches (5 cm) of oil to 375°F (190°C).

While the oil is coming up to temperature, make the sauce: In a small saucepan, combine the Rooster Sauce, vinegar, and honey. Place over medium-high heat and bring to a boil; cook, stirring, until reduced in volume and sticky, about 10 minutes.

Pat the wings dry and put them in a large bowl. Add the cornstarch and toss to evenly coat the wings. Working in batches and using a slotted spoon, add the wings to the oil and fry until crisp and cooked through, 5 to 10 minutes. Remove from the oil using the slotted spoon, drain on paper towels, and immediately season with salt. Transfer to a large bowl as each batch is finished.

Pour the sauce over the wings and toss to coat, then add the butter and scallions and toss until the butter is melted. Serve immediately, with sour cream for dipping if you like.

"...let's get some motherfucking fried chicken up in here once in a while!"

NAME

—TAYSTEE

SISTER INGALLS'S DAILY CORNBREAD

BY   JANE INGALLS

Blueberries or cranberries, whole-wheat or all-purpose flour, I'd be lying if I said I cared. Whatever I can get my hands on works for me! And for me, it's all about the baker man. He had strong hands and long hair when I knew him. Of course that was a long, long time ago. He's probably gone bald by now. He was a Zen monk at Green Gulch Farm near San Francisco. We went for a hike out onto the headlands overlooking Muir beach and ate his cornbread. He was eloquent and knowledgeable. And he didn't smell, which was a bigger issue than you might imagine back in those days. Best of all, he wasn't even Catholic!

MAKES   ONE 10-INCH (25-CM) CORNBREAD

INGREDIENTS

2¼ cups (350 g) medium-grind cornmeal

1 teaspoon baking powder

1 teaspoon baking soda

1 tablespoon sugar (optional)

¾ teaspoon salt

½ cup rapidly boiling water

1½ cups (360 ml) buttermilk

2 large eggs

½ cup (1 stick; 115 g) unsalted butter, cut into pieces

INSTRUCTIONS

Position an oven rack in the middle of the oven, and preheat the oven to 450°F (225°C).

Put a 10-inch (25-cm) cast-iron skillet in the oven for 10 minutes to heat it up (see Note).

Pour ½ cup (80 g) of the cornmeal into a medium bowl.

In a large bowl, combine the remaining 1¾ cups (270 g) cornmeal, the baking powder, baking soda, sugar, if using, and salt.

Pour the boiling water into the reserved ½ cup (80 g) cornmeal and whisk until thick but not firm (it should easily mix into the batter); if it is too firm, add a small amount of additional hot or boiling water. Whisk in the buttermilk, then whisk in the eggs.

Whisk the buttermilk mixture into the dry ingredients. Immediately remove the pan from the oven and add the butter, swirling the pan until the butter is melted. Pour all but 1 tablespoon of the butter into the cornmeal mixture, leaving the remaining butter to grease the pan.

INGREDIENTS

INSTRUCTIONS

Add the batter to the skillet and bake for 12 to 15 minutes, until the edges start to brown, the top begins to crack, and a toothpick inserted in the center comes out clean. Immediately turn out onto a wire rack, cool for a few minutes, then cut into wedges and serve.

NOTE:

Starting with a super-hot skillet ensures a crisp crust; make sure you've got a heavy-duty oven mitt lined up for removing the pan from the oven so you don't forget and grab hold of the handle.

* * * *

CAPUTO: "I saw you yesterday, look the other way when the nun moved a contraband muffin."

FISCHER: "Well, Sister Ingalls is harmless."

CAPUTO: "Sister Ingalls killed a man."

VEE'S

HOMEMADE BREAD

BY YVONNE "VEE" PARKER

The simplicity of a good loaf of homemade bread can be both deceiving and delicious beyond belief. Though the ingredients are common and the directions basic, getting a good product takes time and practice. Making bread is a meditation on nurturing. First the yeast, then the dough, and then finally it grows to become a strong, tasty loaf. While it's often a solitary act, it can bring peace within, even as chaos, anger, and stress swirl around you. But fear not: In the end you will have created something wholesome and comforting that can feed your soul as well as your family.

MAKES 1 LOAF

- 3 tablespoons olive oil, plus more for oiling the bowl and pan
- ¼ cup (60 ml) honey
- 2 cups (240 g) whole-wheat flour
- 1½ cups (190 g) all-purpose flour
- ⅓ cup (50 g) flax seeds
- 1½ teaspoons salt
- 1½ teaspoons instant yeast

In the bowl of an electric mixer fitted with the dough hook, or in a large mixing bowl, combine 1½ cups (360 ml) water and all the ingredients, mixing to form a rough dough. Let the dough rest for 20 minutes, then knead it by machine or by hand for about 10 minutes, until smooth (it will remain a little sticky).

Grease a clean, large bowl with oil and place the dough in the bowl; cover with a clean dish towel and let it rise in a warm place for 1 hour.

Grease an 8½-by-4½-inch (21.5-by-11.5-cm) loaf pan. Shape the dough into a log and place it in the pan, cover with a sheet of lightly oiled plastic wrap, and let it rise for about 1 hour, until it rises about 1 inch (2.5 cm) above the rim of the pan.

Toward the end of the rising time, preheat the oven to 350°F (175°C).

Remove the plastic wrap, place the pan in the oven, and bake for 25 minutes, then tent the loaf with foil and bake for another 25 minutes, or until firm and browned on top. Remove from the oven, turn the bread out of the pan, and place on a wire rack to cool completely before slicing.

BENNETT'S
KALE, DATE, & ALMOND MILK SMOOTHIE

BY JOHN BENNETT

Staying healthy on the job is tough when everything in the cafeteria is fortified with high-fructose corn syrup and comprised of carbs. Being in Litchfield doesn't help either, seeing as how the regional health food store is a mega-chain sandwich shop that has three convenient locations around town. I've found packing your own lunch is the way to go since you're able to control the quality and portions of what you consume. I've been on a real smoothie kick lately. Blend up a big one in the morning and it should last you right up to the afternoon count time. Add a little hot sauce to help suppress hunger. Sweeter fruits tend to hide some of the more bitter greens I add into the smoothie. Not that I have anything to hide . . .

SERVES 1 OR 2
(makes about 2½ cups/540 ml)

- 1½ cups (360 ml) plain unsweetened almond milk

- 4 to 6 dried dates, pitted and cut in half (see Note)

- 1 tablespoon almond butter (optional; for extra protein)

- 1 tablespoon plain whey protein powder (optional)

- 2 cups (50 g) roughly torn kale leaves

- Large pinch of ground ginger

- Large pinch of salt

- 5 or 6 ice cubes

Combine the almond milk, dates, and almond butter, if using, in a blender and blend until smooth. Add the remaining ingredients and blend, starting at low and increasing the speed to high, until smooth.

NOTE: *Soak the dates in the almond milk for an hour before making your smoothie if time allows.*

****

CAPUTO: "Chewing tobacco kind of defeats
the purpose of drinking kale,
doesn't it?"

BENNETT: "I like to think they cancel each other
out, maybe."

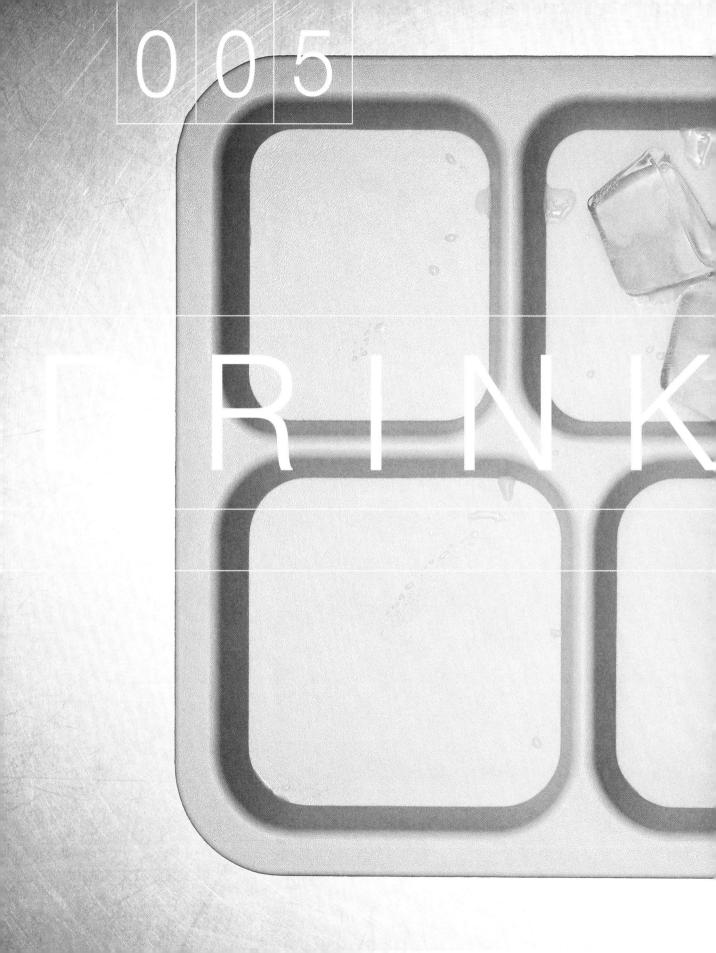

DRINK

S

IN THE CLINK

"I am at a cocktail party on the Upper West Side, drinking Sazeracs..

NAME

—NATALIE "FIG" FIGUEROA

FIG'S
SAZERAC COCKTAIL

BY NATALIE "FIG" FIGUEROA

They've tried to ban it, they've tried to change it, but the Sazerac is America's cocktail. The Sazerac has been around in one form or another going back to before the Civil War. They say an apothecary in the French Quarter of New Orleans used his favorite French brandy to create the original. Then when the Frenchy stuff got expensive, they swapped it out for American rye whiskey and added absinthe. Then absinthe was banned so they began using Herbsaint. So when you drink it, sip it slowly. Inhale the warmth and swallow the burn and think about how this drink has outlasted every other drink of its day. Nothing can take this drink down.

MAKES 1 DRINK

- **Ice cubes (optional)**
- **1 sugar cube**
- **3 dashes of Peychaud's bitters**
- **1 shot rye whiskey**
- **½ teaspoon absinthe or Herbsaint**
- **Twist of lemon peel**

Freeze an Old Fashioned glass for 30 minutes or pack it with ice to chill it.

In a second Old Fashioned glass, combine the sugar cube and bitters and crush the sugar cube. Add the whiskey.

Remove the first glass from the freezer or discard the ice if you used it. Add the absinthe to the cold glass; swirl it around to coat the sides and bottom of the glass. Pour out the excess.

Pour the whiskey mixture into the chilled glass and serve, garnished with the lemon peel.

LUSCHEK'S

HOT CHOCOLATE & SCHNAPPS

BY JOEL LUSCHEK

That coffee company was right when they said the worst part of waking up is a hangover in a freezing apartment. I'm pretty sure that's how it goes. It's been happening daily, since my roommate and I haven't paid the gas bill in two months. There's barely enough time for me to shower, so I'll throw on whatever uniform is the cleanest and spray on some deodorant until the smell of cigarettes and stale beer are covered up, or at least masked. There's a coffee place up the street that I stop at every morning. It's got a drive-thru, so that means I don't really have to face other human beings at such an ungodly hour (and it's easier to not tip without getting the evil eye). A warm seasonal beverage with some of Grandpa's old cough medicine I keep in the glove box and I'm ready to face a bunch of angry women.

MAKES 2 MUGSFUL

- **1½ cups (360 ml) whole milk**
- **½ cup (120 ml) heavy cream**
- **1 ounce (30 ml) cinnamon or peppermint schnapps**
- **Large pinch of ground cayenne**
- **3 ounces (85 g) bittersweet chocolate, coarsely chopped**

In a medium saucepan, combine the milk, cream, schnapps, and cayenne. Place over medium heat and bring to a simmer. Remove the pan from the heat, add the chocolate, and let stand until melted. Whisk until smooth, then pour into mugs and serve.

BIG HOUSE BUGLE

1st Edition   "All the Lowdown on the Litch"   Page 1

GUARDS, THEY'RE PEOPLE TOO!

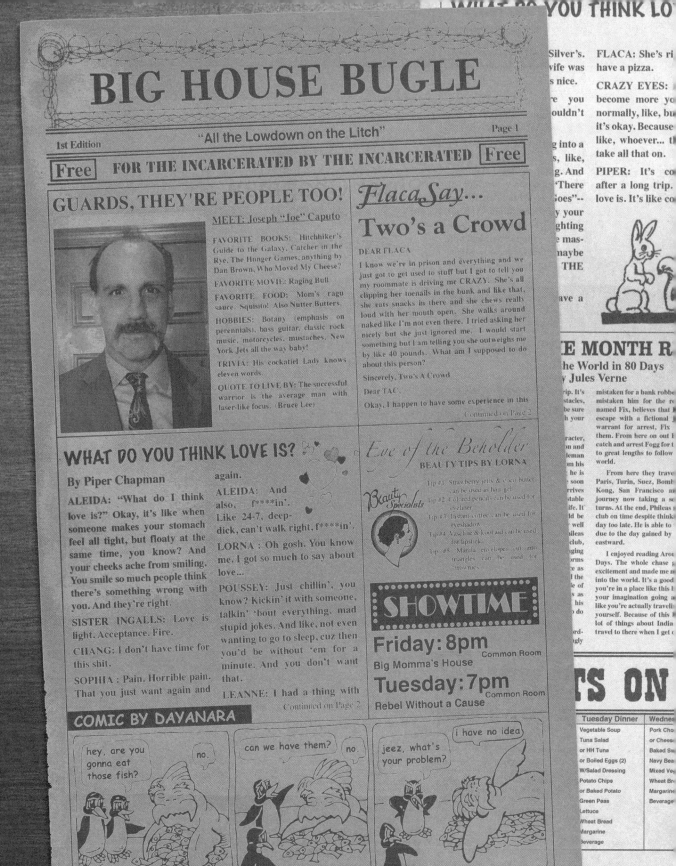

MEET: Joseph "Joe" Caputo

FAVORITE BOOKS: Hitchhiker's Guide to the Galaxy, Catcher in the Rye, The Hunger Games, anything by Dan Brown, Who Moved My Cheese?

FAVORITE MOVIE: Raging Bull

FAVORITE FOOD: Mom's ragu sauce. Squisito! Also Nutter Butters.

HOBBIES: Botany (emphasis on perennials), bass guitar, classic rock music, motorcycles, mustaches, New York Jets all the way baby!

TRIVIA: His cockatiel Lady knows eleven words.

QUOTE TO LIVE BY: The successful warrior is the average man with laser-like focus. (Bruce Lee)

Flaca Say...
Two's a Crowd

DEAR FLACA

I know we're in prison and everything and we just got to get used to stuff but I got to tell you my roommate is driving me CRAZY. She's all clipping her toenails in the bunk and like that, she eats snacks in there and she chews really loud with her mouth open. She walks around naked like I'm not even there. I tried asking her nicely but she just ignored me. I would start something but I am telling you she outweighs me by like 40 pounds. What am I supposed to do about this person?

Sincerely, Two's A Crowd

Dear TAC,

Okay, I happen to have some experience in this

Continued on Page 2

WHAT DO YOU THINK LOVE IS?

By Piper Chapman

ALEIDA: "What do I think love is?" Okay, it's like when someone makes your stomach feel all tight, but floaty at the same time, you know? And your cheeks ache from smiling. You smile so much people think there's something wrong with you. And they're right.

SISTER INGALLS: Love is light. Acceptance. Fire.

CHANG: I don't have time for this shit.

SOPHIA : Pain. Horrible pain. That you just want again and

again.

ALEIDA: And also, f****in'. Like 24-7, deep-dick, can't walk right, f****in'.

LORNA : Oh gosh. You know me, I got so much to say about love...

POUSSEY: Just chillin', you know? Kickin' it with someone, talkin' 'bout everything, mad stupid jokes. And like, not even wanting to go to sleep, cuz then you'd be without 'em for a minute. And you don't want that.

LEANNE: I had a thing with

Continued on Page 2

Eye of the Beholder
BEAUTY TIPS BY LORNA

Beauty Specialists

Tip #1: Strawberry jelly & coco butter can be used as hair gel

Tip #2: Colored pencils can be used for eyeliner

Tip #3: Instant coffee can be used for eyeshadow

Tip #4: Vaseline & Kool aid can be used for lipstick

Tip #5: Manila envelopes cut into triangles can be used for brownies

SHOWTIME

Friday: 8pm   Common Room
Big Momma's House

Tuesday: 7pm   Common Room
Rebel Without a Cause

COMIC BY DAYANARA

hey, are you gonna eat those fish?

no.

can we have them?

no.

jeez, what's your problem?

i have no idea

(partial adjacent page)

Silver's. wife was nice.

re you ouldn't

g into a s, like, g. And 'There oes"-- y your ghting e mas- maybe THE

ve a

FLACA: She's ri have a pizza.

CRAZY EYES: become more yo normally, like, bu it's okay. Because like, whoever... t take all that on.

PIPER: It's co after a long trip. love is. It's like co

MONTH R
he World in 80 Days
y Jules Verne

rip. It's stacles, be sure h your

racter, on and leman om his he is soon rrives table life. It d be well hileas club, nging rms e as the le of s as his o do

rd- ngly

mistaken for a bank robbe mistaken him for the r named Fix, believes that escape with a fictional warrant for arrest, Fix them. From here on out catch and arrest Fogg for to great lengths to follow world.

From here they trave Paris, Turin, Suez, Bomb Kong, San Francisco a journey now taking a s turns. At the end, Phileas club on time despite thinki day too late. He is able to due to the day gained by eastward.

I enjoyed reading Arou Days. The whole chase excitement and made me into the world. It's a good you're in a place like this your imagination going a like you're actually travell yourself. Because of this lot of things about India travel to there when I get

TS ON

Tuesday Dinner	Wednes
Vegetable Soup	Pork Cho
Tuna Salad	or Cheese
or HH Tuna	Baked Sw
or Boiled Eggs (2)	Navy Bea
W/Salad Dressing	Mixed Ve
Potato Chips	Wheat Br
or Baked Potato	Margarine
Green Peas	Beverage
Lettuce	
Wheat Bread	
Margarine	
Beverage	

Two's a Crowd

Continued from Page 1

department because when I first got here I had a
bunkie who had severe b.o., like I felt like the
inside of my nostrils was burning, you know
what I'm saying? And I tried to be ⬚⬚⬚⬚⬚⬚
at first, like dropping hints and stuff⬚
started to get pretty straight-up about⬚
about it but man, it was like she just⬚
a [expletive deleted]. So here's wh⬚
did, and you can do it too but you ge⬚
to it or it won't work, you got to act⬚
she is until she gets scared of yo⬚
nothing against the prison rules ⬚
because those rules are there for a re⬚
everybody safe (Hi, Mr. Caputo!) ⬚
rocking out to real loud music in⬚
except there's no music playing, ⬚
good one is, pretend like you got an⬚
cat that only you can see. And it⬚
health crisises and stuff and yo⬚
telling her about it. You can come⬚
own ideas too. The important t⬚
woman needs to fear you. Not a ⬚
going to need to defend herself, ju⬚
she doesn't want to piss you off, yo⬚
I'm saying. Okay, try that and if it⬚
get back to me and I will think of so⬚
Peace.

The ABC's of Y⬚
By Yoga Jones

Unlock the door to your imagination⬚
of the ladies here like to imagin⬚
windows opening. Wide blue skie⬚
king cone. Whatever will get you ⬚
place.

Now we can begin our medi⬚

Deep breath in. Exhale out. Dee⬚
Exhale out Deep breath in. E⬚

Akasha

Amrita

Arjuna

The cow jumped over the ⬚

Brahmana

Bhakta

Bandha

This has become my ma⬚

Cin-mudra

Cin-midra

Chakra

The doors in here all l⬚

Breath and repeat.

Yoga class is 2 times a day at Noon and⬚

E MENU⬚

⬚ursday Dinner	Friday Dinner	
⬚ked Ziti	Baked Meatloaf	⬚
⬚H Ziti & Beef	or HH Meatloaf	⬚
⬚oy Baked Ziti	or Soy Burger	⬚
⬚nach	W/Salad Dressing	M⬚
⬚den Salad	Mashed Potatoes	⬚
⬚Dressing, Reg & Diet	or HH Mashed Potato	R⬚
⬚ic Bread	Brown Gravy	or⬚
⬚Wheat Bread (1)	WK Corn	M⬚
⬚garine	Wheat Bread (1)	⬚
⬚verage	Margarine	⬚
	Beverage	N⬚

BIG HOUSE BUGLE

2nd Edition — "All the Lowdown on the Litch" — Page 1

Free — FOR THE INCARCERATED BY THE INCARCERATED — **Free**

GUARDS, THEY'RE PEOPLE TOO!

S. Fischer — Federal Department of Corrections

Meet: Susan Fischer

Favorite Books: "G" is for Gumshoe, Forever, Jane Eyre, Bossypants, Little Women, The Help

Favorite Movie: You've Got Mail

Favorite Food: Mint Milanos, Chop Suey

Hobbies: Knitting, Intramural Softball, Mentoring at Litchfield Elementary, Archery, Karaoke

Trivia: She won her fifth grade district Geography Bee and is fluent in Spanish

Quote to Live by: "The aim for me is making people feel like they're not alone." -Zooey Deschanel

CRITIC'S CORNER

Grease
By Nicky Nichols

"Grease is the word" claims the opening song in the film version of the musical yet the word is never really said in the movie. While it's filled with a bunch of catchy songs and some good dance scenes from Mr. Scientology himself John Travolta, it's the film's overall message that really bothers me.

"Grease" is the story of two star-crossed lovers, Danny Zuko and Sandy (I don't know her last name), who, after spending a summer either hanging on the boardwalk or having sex in the sand (there are conflicting stories), parted ways never to see each other again. Until one day, they run into each other at a pep rally (what the Greasers are doing there, I still have no idea). Danny tries to act all cool in front of his friend and comes off like a jerk. This part in the movie is super realistic as men are jerks and only try to impress their friends. There was this one guy named Luis who would come over after school and we'd get frisky and he'd say how much he liked me and then I'd try to sit with him at lunch and him and his friends would laugh at my Lisa Frank Trapper Keeper.

Anyway, Danny and Sandy try to start up their relationship again but they're just too different. Sandy is a goodie two shoes and Danny is a bad boy who loves to sing and dance (confusing, I know). The Greasers give Danny a hard time for not sealing the deal with Sandy, because

Continued on Page 2

SHOWTIME

Friday: 8pm Common Room
Joe Versus The Volcano

Tuesday: 7pm Common Room
Rebel Without a Cause

Flaca Say...
To Catch A Thief

Dear Flaca,

My Bunkie is lifting my shit, how should I handle the situation? For the past few weeks, things have been disappearing from my bunk. I thought I was going crazy, misplacing things, maybe sleepwalking (my brother used to sleepwalk as a kid and put pillows in the oven or shove Oreos in the VCR). Then one day, I'm coming back from the showers and I see my bunkie putting my mascara in her pocket. I didn't know what to say (I hate confrontation)but she's lifting my shit. What would you do in this situation?

Angrily, To Catch A Thief

Dear TCAT,

Try to reason with that bitch to lay off the sticky fingers, but if she keeps it up, take her to a secluded spot, away from the COs and bash her head real good.

Three Ways To Get A Man To Like You
By Lorna Morello

#1) Men like to be in control and be protective. It is an instinct that goes back millions of years to when we were apes. All you have to do is make them feel you need their protection. You have to ask for their help, which can be difficult for some ladies. Be sure to wear soft clothes and pastel colors which really make a man feel like you're in need of protection.

#2) Men also want to feel ⬚⬚⬚⬚'t w⬚ be a burden. Don't alwa⬚⬚⬚ wants to meet. If he asks y⬚⬚⬚ then hang out after, tell him you⬚ about the next night? And if he doesn⬚ be jealous.

#3) More than anything, men want to⬚ and have the last word. You can make⬚ very knowledgeable by asking them ⬚ about themselves. If you know they a⬚ don't tell them. If you know the answer, ⬚ it. Let them be right.

Look at the beautiful new pen I built you!

Hey! She's hogging all the space for herself!

FOR PIGS ONLY

CAPUTO'S GARDENING TIPS

* *

WHAT ARE YOU GOING TO GROW?

* Try not to bite off more than you can chew with your first garden.
  It's better to have a small, beautifully complex and vibrant garden
  than a large field of dying plants.
* Learning what grows well where you live takes time, trial, and
  error. Choose several options from different types of plants,
  annual and perennial flowers, bulbs and seeds, vegetables and herbs.
  Then experiment.

WHERE ARE YOU GOING TO GROW?

* When choosing what you will grow, you should take into consideration where you will be putting your garden.
* How much sun does your plot get? What time of day does it get it? Will it be blocked when the path of the sun changes midseason behind the large oak tree? All these things matter, because the right amount of sun is important.
* Once you've marked out your plot, you need to prepare the soil as well. Most soil is not fertile enough and needs to be added to and improved with planting soil or compost.

HOW DO YOU PLANT PLANTS?

* Once you have the soil in your plot ready, you need to lay out the plants. First you need to check how far apart they need to be. This can be deceiving to the beginner's eye, but you must imagine the plant growing much larger and remember it needs as much room below the ground as above the ground, if not more.
* To get a sense of where everything will fit, I often put each seedling out in its spot and then dig the hole for each one.
* Make sure you don't dig too deep, but also be sure the holes are not too shallow. Every plant needs the right balance.
* If you are planting bulbs, make sure you plant them right side up. (I've made this mistake myself when I was starting out with tulips.)

HOW DO YOU KEEP PLANTS ALIVE?

* Caring for a plant is all about balance and patience.
* You must water plants regularly, but you don't want to overwater. If the soil feels wet, then it's likely you should not be watering.
* The same balance needs to be considered when fertilizing the soil. Plants need strong soil, but if you put in too much Miracle-Gro you will change the chemicals in the soil and the plants won't make it.
* Most importantly, don't be impatient. Plants need time to grow just as gardeners need time to learn. It could be several seasons before you've got a hang of it, but it's well worth it.
* Don't give up!

PORNSTACHE SHOOTER

BY GEORGE MENDEZ

After a tough day of kicking ass and taking names, me and the boys (well . . . at least Bennett) hit the local watering hole. Order a couple of boilermakers to get the night started from my bartender pal, who I call "bartender." He calls me "pal." He's hilarious. Suddenly, I notice my little buddy (I'm talking about Bennett, not my dick) sees a few attractive townies, so we send over drinks courtesy of moi. These bitches have the nerve to send them back. Fine, more for us. Someone once said, "I drink to make other people interesting." You're goddamn right.

MAKES 1 SHOOTER

- **1 ounce (30 ml) cold vodka**
- **1 cold raw oyster, including juices**
- **Dash of hot sauce**
- **Wedge of lemon**

Pour the vodka into a shot glass and add the oyster juices. Add the hot sauce and stir. Drop in the oyster, bite the lemon, and swallow.

VARIATION

"BLOODY" PORNSTACHE SHOOTER:
Add ½ ounce (15 ml) tomato juice, a dash of prepared horseradish, and a couple shakes of Worcestershire sauce.

"Are you serious? That's the first thing you say to me,
buy us a fuckin' drink? Do you believe these fuckin' sluts, Bennett?"

— PORNSTACHE

"...I'm a human being, man.

I'm a person, you know, with feelings and emotions.
Does anybody ever ask me how my day is going?"

NAME

—GEORGE "PORNSTACHE" MENDEZ

POUSSEY'S HOOCH

BY POUSSEY WASHINGTON
BY . . . .

Sometimes, during long nights in here, I get to thinking about how my moms loved Oktoberfest. I never saw her drink a beer back home, but when we moved to Germany my dad took us out to the festival near the base at Ramstein where they really do it up. They got wine, beer, brats. They even got polka music up in there. Mom loved it so much she made my pops wear one of those hats and she got one of those funny dresses that looks like a sexy maid outfit. And she looked good, too. All those white-ass German dudes checking her out were like, "Damn, look at this fine African lady. Can I touch your hair?" Lucky for them my mom didn't understand German. And 'cause it's legal for kids to drink there, she let me have a beer even though I was only fourteen. She always cared about following the law more than I did.

HOWEVER MUCH YOU CAN GET YOUR HANDS ON
MAKES . . . .

INGREDIENTS

GINGER BEER HOOCH

1 part moonshine

2 parts ginger beer

Squeeze of lime juice

COLA HOOCH

1 part moonshine

2 parts cola

Squeeze of lime juice

MISSING SCREWDRIVER HOOCH

1 part moonshine

4 parts orange juice

SLAMMER SLAMMER

1 part moonshine

1 part fruit juice

HARDCORE HOOCH

1 part moonshine

1 part moonshine

INSTRUCTIONS

Combine the ingredients and serve over ice, if you've got it.

VARIATION

HELLFIRE HOOCH: Steep a handful of chiles in a bottle of hooch for a week. Then give the chiles to Piper to chew on.

LITCHFIELD
CORRECTIONAL
INSTITUTION

NAME WASHINGTON POUSSEY
　　　　LAST　　　　　　　　　FIRST

ALIAS

NUMBER 1147-5609　　　　SEX F　RACE Black

NCIC NUMBER

LEAVE BLANK

FINGER PRINT CLASSIFICATION

RIGHT HAND

| Index | Middle | Ring | Little |

LEFT HAND

| Index | Middle | Ring | Little |

PRISON PUNCH DEVIATIONS

BY . . . .
LEANNE TAYLOR

I never understood milk. It's gross. I'm okay with strawberry milk I guess, cause
that's sweet, but regular milk is disgusting. My mama says even when I was a little
baby, I would always swat away her tit. Growing up she never let me have sugary
drinks. I remember the first time I snuck into Cici's Pizza I mixed up a graveyard at
the soda fountain. Every single flavor (except root beer, it's too strong and throws
off the flavor profile). The closest we ever get to that inside is some prison punch
which is a mixture of fruit juice concentrate and some flat soda. When I get out, the
first thing I'm gonna do is go to a 7-11 and drown myself even if I gotta use root beer.

MAKES . . . .
HOWEVER MUCH YOU CAN GET YOUR HANDS ON

INGREDIENTS	INSTRUCTIONS
KOOL-AID PUNCH 4 parts sweetened Kool-Aid, any flavor 1 part moonshine	Combine the ingredients and stir to dissolve the Kool-Aid. Serve over ice if you've got it. **NOTE:** Save the leftover cherry Kool-Aid to trade with Sophia.
PICKLE PUNCH 1 part pickle juice 1 part moonshine	Combine the ingredients and serve over ice if you've got it.
JAILHOUSE RELIEF ¼ teaspoon unsweetened cherry Kool-Aid powder 4 ounces (120 ml) moonshine 4 teaspoons sugar	Combine the ingredients and stir to dissolve the Kool-Aid and sugar. Serve over ice if you've got it.

AN EXCERPT FROM DAYA'S PREGNANCY JOURNAL

****

Week 1 . . . . . . I think somethin's weird. I keep gettin' sick in the mornin'. Can't keep anything down, which sucks 'cause I love the new type of tamarind candy they got at commissary. Heartburn's a bitch, too. Poppin' Tums like they're Smarties.

Week 2 . . . . . . Oh shit . . . I'm late. I wonder what John is gonna say. . . . Babies behind bars. Great job, Daya. I guess the apple don't fall far from the branch.

Week 4 . . . . . . God, I just want to poop. This ain't even funny. I ain't gone in days. I been drinkin' pineapple soda nonstop but still nothin'. I gotta see if Gloria can get me some prunes or somethin'.

Week 7 . . . . . . All I want are Doritos. I don't care what flavor. I used to date this dude in high school who would never buy a big bag of Doritos. He'd always get four different little bags and pour 'em into a Ziploc bag. He called it his "party bag" 'cause you never know which flavor you gonna get.

Week 9 . . . . . . I been eatin' lemons this week. Like straight-up whole lemons. I can't get enough of that sour shit. It's like those sour candies from when you were a kid and you'd compete to see who could keep a straight face the longest. I'd kick so much ass at that game now.

Week 10 . . . . . My nipples been stickin' out all the time. I gotta add toilet paper to my bra to hide those things. Been sneakin' out little cups of pickle juice from the kitchen. Always thought that pickle stuff was just in the movies, but damn, it be for real. Can't get enough salt. Best part about workin' there is that I can satisfy almost any craving I got without anyone noticing.

NAME   DIAZ, DAYANARA

NUMBER   1278-1820

LABOR-INDUCING PINEAPPLE SODA

BY . . . . ALEIDA DIAZ

It ain't rocket algebra to know that five kids gets you loose down there. We're talkin', the baby practically falls out you when it's ready. First-time moms need a little extra help, though. Some say spicy food gets that baby going, some swear by the old hot and heavy (but that's what got you into trouble in the first place, and it's hard to come by in here!). I usually go for pineapples. They're delicious, refreshing, and make mi prima blow up 'cause she's allergic. Stuff is hilarious at parties. If your man is still around, make him go to the store and stock up. You're gonna want it when you feel like a water balloon that just can't pop.

MAKES . . . . ABOUT 1 CUP (240 ML) SYRUP, FOR 4 TO 6 SODAS

INGREDIENTS

2 cups (480 ml) unsweetened pineapple juice, preferably Lotus Pineapple Juice from Puerto Rico

½ cup (100 g) sugar

Seltzer water

Fresh or candied red chile slices (optional)

INSTRUCTIONS

Pour the pineapple juice into a medium saucepan and add the sugar. Place over high heat and bring to a boil, stirring to dissolve the sugar. Boil until the pineapple juice is darkened in color and thickened but not quite syrupy, about 20 minutes. Remove the pan from the heat whenever the juice starts to foam vigorously and threatens to rise out of the pan; return to the heat once the foam subsides. Let cool completely and transfer to a bottle. For each soda, put 3 to 4 tablespoons of the pineapple syrup (depending on how sweet you like it and how fast you'd like to induce labor) into a glass. Fill the glass with about 1 cup of seltzer and stir to dissolve the syrup. Serve immediately with ice, and with red chile slices if desired.

NAME...
LAST FIRST

DIAZ   ALEIDA

NUMBER... SEX........... RACE...................

1854-8780   F   Hispanic

NICKY'S MOSCOW MULE

BY . . . .
NICKY NICHOLS

No class out there anymore. Last time I ordered a Moscow Mule the barman, who looked like he was twenty-one and three quarters, had to admit he'd never heard of the drink. I said, "Are you joking? This was the drink that brought vodka to the thirsty American masses." Clearly, it's time for a refresher on this refreshing cocktail. The drink came about through what some might call typical American ingenuity. Others might call it bullshit. One guy was struggling to sell his ginger beer, another guy had more copper mugs than he knew what to do with, and a third guy decided he'd throw in some limes and vodka and get hammered. Turned into one of the most popular cocktails of the '50s and '60s. So if you're looking to class it up, or get in good with Red, learn to make a Moscow Mule, and God help you if you try to substitute ginger ale for ginger beer.

MAKES . . . .
1 DRINK

INGREDIENTS

Ice cubes

2 ounces (60 ml) vodka

1 lime wedge

4 to 6 ounces (120 to 180 ml) cold ginger beer, preferably Cock 'n Bull brand

1 fresh mint sprig (optional)

INSTRUCTIONS

Throw a couple ice cubes into a Collins glass or copper Moscow Mule mug. Add the vodka, squeeze in the juice from the lime, and throw the wedge into the glass. Fill with the ginger beer, garnish with the mint sprig, if using, and serve.

VARIATIONS

MEXICAN MULE: Substitute tequila for the vodka.

LIBRE MULE: Substitute cola for the ginger beer.

HOW TO MAKE A LITCHFIELD LIGHTER

By Nicky Nichols

****

1) Get a piece of gum with a foil wrapper. Eat piece of gum.

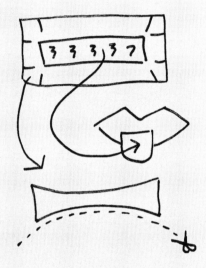

2) This part gets tricky. You need to cut the wrapper into an hourglass shape so there's just the slightest bit of foil connecting the larger parts of the wrapper.

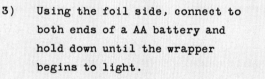

3) Using the foil side, connect to both ends of a AA battery and hold down until the wrapper begins to light.

4) The light goes fast, so get your smoke ready.

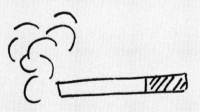

5) Enjoy your cigarette in peace. But don't let a CO catch you.

PIPER'S
CLEANSE

BY PIPER CHAPMAN

Juicing with a healthy, toxin-flushing cleanse, when you're at home, is fantastic and relaxing. It makes your cheekbones jut out, and everyone comments on how great you look after you start to lose weight. You have to drink lots of fluids, you have to lay low, and you have to be near a bathroom. Do not try to juice if you're traveling. I once tried to lose weight while staying in Prague. You never know when you're gonna need a bathroom, and nothing is harder to find in Prague than a toilet. Except maybe a laundromat, which, if you fail to find a toilet in time, you're definitely gonna need.

MAKES 1 DRINK

- **10 ounces (300 ml) filtered warm or room-temperature water**
- **2 tablespoons organic maple syrup**
- **2 tablespoons fresh lemon juice**
- **Pinch of ground cayenne**

In a glass, combine all the ingredients, stir, and drink.

NOTE: The original recipe for the Master Cleanse can be found in the book The Master Cleanser, *by Stanley Burroughs.*

"When you said 'cleanse,' I thought you meant
we'd be eating more kale."

— LARRY

NAME..
          LAST

VAUSE   ALEX

NUMBER..   SEX.............   RACE...............

1975-0425   F   White

DOWN & DIRTY MARGARITA

BY ALEX VAUSE

When I order a margarita I want it strong and I want it cold. When you're pretty and you're a girl, people go light with the booze. I say fuck that girly shit. Give me the industrial-strength drink, 'cause I can handle it. I used to drink margaritas on my trips. I would walk past customs agents with over a hundred thousand in my bag. I always stayed cool, even with ten keys of heroin in my suitcase while a dog sniffed and barked. No problem. It was the fourteen or fifteen hours on the plane beforehand, imagining all the scenarios, imagining your life in prison, imagining losing everything you love: That's when I really needed that margarita.

MAKES 1 DRINK

- **Salt**

- **1 lime wedge plus a couple of slices**

- **1 green olive (optional)**

- **Ice cubes**

- **1 shot tequila**

- **1 shot orange juice or Cointreau**

- **½ shot fresh lime juice**

- **½ teaspoon olive juice from the jar, or to taste**

Pour enough salt on a small plate to cover it. Rub the lime wedge onto the outside of a cocktail glass to moisten it. Hold the glass upside down and dip the rim in the salt.

Throw the olive in the glass, if using. Fill a cocktail shaker with ice. Add the tequila, orange juice, lime juice, and olive juice. Shake the cocktail shaker vigorously until the drink becomes frosty, then strain the drink into the glass, garnish with the lime slices, and serve.

LONG ISLAND ICED TEA

BY MARISOL "FLACA" GONZALES

When my girls and me used to roll up to the club, the bouncer would look us up and down and go, "Daaaamn!" We'd pass through that velvet rope and leave all those feas behind. Mis chicas have a rule: We buy one drink, then we find some guy with bottle service and plant ourselves at his table. The drink of choice at La Biblioteca in the Bronx is the Long Island Iced Tea, 'cause that shit is fuerte and cheap as hell. You know they put like nine different kinds of booze in there? Start the night off with one of those bad boys and you'll be on the dance floor makin' that booty clap for the man of your dreams. Those were the days.

MAKES 1 DRINK

- **1 bottle Mexican beer, such as Dos Equis**
- **1 shot tequila**
- **1 lime slice**

Pour the beer into a pint glass and add the tequila. Garnish with the lime slice.

TRADITIONAL LONG ISLAND ICED TEA

MAKES 2 DRINKS

- **Ice cubes**
- **1 ounce (30 ml) vodka**
- **1 ounce (30 ml) gin**
- **1 ounce (30 ml) white rum**
- **1 ounce (30 ml) white tequila**
- **1 ounce (30 ml) triple sec**
- **1 ounce (30 ml) orange juice**
- **½ cup (120 ml) cola**
- **2 lemon or orange wedges**

Fill a cocktail shaker with ice. Pour the vodka, gin, rum, tequila, triple sec, and orange juice into the shaker. Cover and shake vigorously to mix and chill the liquors. Pour the mixture including the ice into two glasses and top them off with the cola. Garnish with the lemon wedges and serve.

RICO COLADA

BY GLORIA MENDOZA

New York gets cold. I'm not just talking about the weather. Although once I had to walk home from Manhattan across the Brooklyn Bridge in February after I lost my wallet, and that shit was fuckin' freezing. I'm talking about how you never get a moment to rest in the city. You're on your feet from dawn until dark. But what can you do? You want a island vacation? No way. You're gonna bust your ass till your ass is busted. But that's why you need to mix up a piña colada. That rum and coconut and pineapple hits your taste buds and makes you feel like you're on a perfect beach with the waves crashing. And if you have three in a row you'll love New York like a tourist.

MAKES 2 DRINKS

- **Ice cubes**
- **2 shots spiced rum**
- **2 shots coconut rum**
- **½ shot grenadine or Chambord**
- **4 shots orange juice or pineapple juice**
- **1 pineapple wedge and/or maraschino cherry (optional)**

Fill a tall glass with ice. Add the spiced rum, coconut rum, and grenadine and top with the orange juice. Stir, and serve with the pineapple wedge and/or maraschino cherry if you've got them.

TRADITIONAL PIÑA COLADA

MAKES 1 DRINK

- **½ cup (120 ml) pineapple juice**
- **¼ cup (120 ml) white, dark, or coconut rum**
- **2 tablespoons canned sweetened cream of coconut**
- **½ cup ice**
- **4 pineapple wedges and/or maraschino cherries (optional)**

In a blender, combine the pineapple juice, rum, cream of coconut, and ice and blend on high speed until the ice is crushed and the drink is smooth, about 30 seconds. Pour into a glass and serve, with the pineapple wedge and maraschino cherry if you like.

GLORIA'S SANTERIA RITUALS

* *

* <u>To remove a neighbor's evil eye:</u>
> Tie a red ribbon around a bunch of
> bananas. Hang them from the roof of
> your house until rotten. They will
> absorb all of your neighbor's envy.

* <u>To drive away an unpleasant person:</u>
> Take hairs from the head of a dog
> or a cat. Toast them and pulverize
> them. Blow the powder on the
> unwanted person.

* <u>To drive away illness:</u>
> Tie a dry corn cob behind the door
> with a purple ribbon.

* <u>To keep the police away:</u>
> Grind sage leaves into a powder
> and blow on your door.

* <u>To have good luck:</u>
> Cover a white bed sheet with laurel
> leaves. Sleep on them.

* <u>To keep your house free of spirits:</u>
> Don't rock empty rocking chairs.

* * * *

*"Yeah and I'd give my left tit for a piña colada
and a smoke, but you don't see that on the menu . . . "*

— GLORIA

RT

FOR GOOD BEHAVIOR

DESERT STORM PUDDING

UNITED STATES MILITARY, FOOD SERVICES DIVISION

BY..

CONTENTS: American-Style Vanilla Pudding

MEAL TYPE: Dessert

DESCRIPTION: After a tough day on the battlefield, it's good to come back to base camp for some of the comforts of home. With the U.S. Military's American-Style Vanilla Pudding, you'll experience pudding-type flavor like Mom used to make. In conjunction with other U.S. Military food products, our soldiers are provided with the diet they need to keep them in tip-top fighting shape. God bless our troops and the United States of America.

USE BY: 3/14/1993

SERVES.....4...

INGREDIENTS

2/3 cup (120 g) sugar

3 tablespoons cornstarch

1/8 teaspoon salt

2 1/4 cups (530 ml) whole milk

Seeds from 2 vanilla beans (see Note), or 1 tablespoon vanilla extract

3 large egg yolks

1/2 cup (120 ml) heavy cream

3 tablespoons unsalted butter, cut into pieces

INSTRUCTIONS

In a medium saucepan, combine the sugar, cornstarch, and salt. Whisk in the milk and vanilla seeds, if using, place over medium heat, and heat, whisking occasionally, until almost simmering.

Meanwhile, in a large bowl, whisk the egg yolks with the cream; slowly whisk about 1 cup (240 ml) of the hot milk mixture into the egg mixture, then slowly whisk the egg mixture into the saucepan. Cook, whisking constantly, until the mixture comes to a simmer, then reduce the heat to medium-low and simmer, continuing to whisk constantly, until the pudding starts to thicken and ribbons form when you lift the whisk and drizzle a bit of pudding over the surface, about 10 minutes.

Remove from the heat and whisk in the butter and vanilla extract, if using, until the butter is completely melted. Pour through a fine-mesh strainer into a large bowl or individual serving bowls. If you are not a pudding skin lover, press a piece of plastic wrap directly over the surface of the pudding. Let cool completely, then refrigerate until cold, about 2 hours, before serving.

(continued)

Desert Storm Pudding (cont.)

RECIPE

INGREDIENTS

INSTRUCTIONS

NOTE:

To remove vanilla seeds from the pods, use the back of a paring knife to cut a horizontal slit through the beans and scrape out the seeds. (Pre-prison Piper might have tossed the spent beans into a jar of sugar and left it for 1 to 2 weeks to make vanilla sugar.)

VARIATIONS

CHOCOLATE-VANILLA OR VANILLA-VANILLA PUDDING: Top with chocolate chips or whipped cream according to your preference.

VANILLA-CHOCOLATE OR CHOCOLATE-CHOCOLATE PUDDING: Add 3 tablespoons cocoa powder when you add the cornstarch. Top the pudding with crumbled vanilla wafers or chocolate chips.

See page 192 for more swirly-mix dessert options.

PIPER'S BOOK CLUB VANILLA PUDDING WITH ROSEWATER-SCENTED BERRIES: Combine 1 pint (170 g) fresh raspberries with 1 tablespoon sugar and 1 teaspoon rosewater. Squeeze in the juice of ½ lemon, toss, and let sit for 30 minutes to macerate, tossing a few times. Top bowls of pudding with the raspberries.

IT IS MANDATORY
THAT ALL MESS
HALL WORKERS
WEAR A HAIRNET AT
ALL TIMES WHILE
WORKING IN THE
MESS HALL !!!!!!!!!!

ALL FOODS
MUST BE COVERED

"Surviving here is all about perspective.
Don't eat the pudding. It comes in big cans
marked 'Desert Storm.'"

NAME

—YOGA JONES

NAME   JONES   ERICA
        LAST   FIRST

NUMBER   1260-9865   SEX F   RACE   White

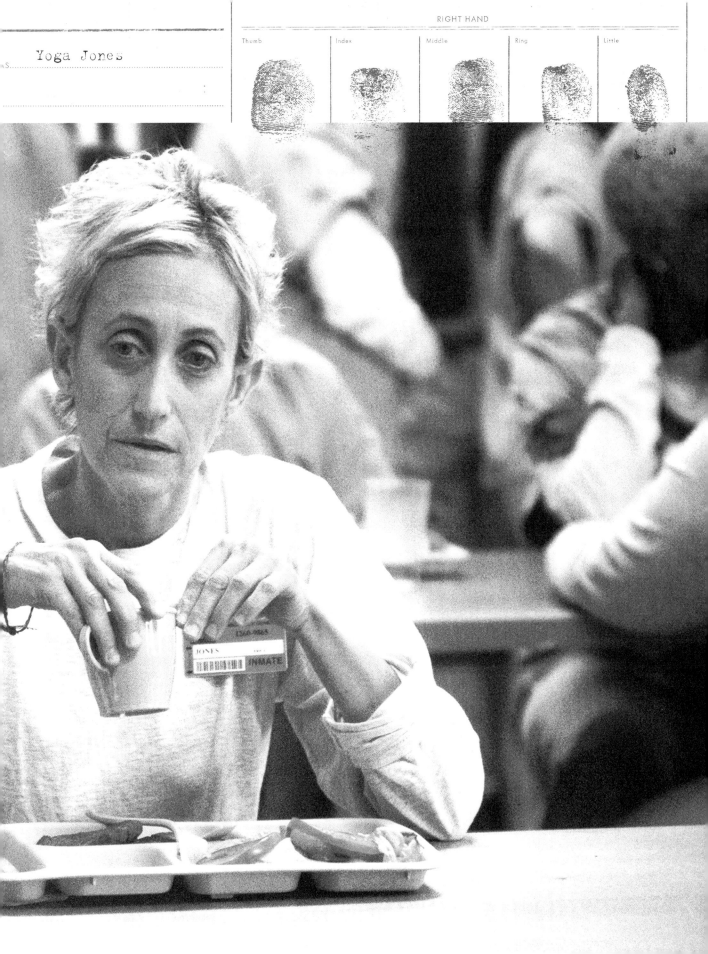

Yoga Jones

AS.

JONES   INMATE

CRAZY EYES'S CHOCOLATE AND VANILLA FUDGE SWIRL (Swirrl, Swirrl)

BY .... **SUZANNE WARREN**

I wish we could get a soft serve machine in Litchfield. A lot of toppings, too. Strawberries, cookie crumbles, jimmies, maybe some pineapple when I'm feeling like having a luau in my mind. The greatest topping, without a doubt, is gummy bears. Now, alone, they're delicious, but once they hit the soft serve, they begin to harden up. Suddenly, your mouth is on a mission to destroy the gummy bears, but they won't give up without a fight. They get tough, and eating them is so much fun. I don't really like chocolate and I don't really like vanilla, but when they're together, two flavors become one and it's magic, chocolate and vanilla swirling together to create a truly sublime taste. What a way for those gummy bears to go. When I'm in need of my swirl, these days, the fudge in the cafeteria keeps me going, but I sure will miss those bears.

MAKES .... **36 PIECES**

INGREDIENTS

Butter for the pan

¾ cup (180 ml) evaporated milk

1¾ cups (350 g) sugar

½ teaspoon salt

1½ cups (150 g) mini marshmallows

2 teaspoons vanilla extract

1½ cups (250 g) semisweet or milk chocolate chips

½ cup (55 g) chopped pecans or walnuts

More chocolate chips or mini marshmallows for topping

INSTRUCTIONS

Line a 9-inch (23-cm) baking pan with foil so that it extends up the sides and over the edges of the pan. Grease the foil with butter.

In a large saucepan, whisk together the evaporated milk, sugar, and salt. Bring to a boil over medium-high heat and boil, stirring constantly, for 5 minutes, or until the mixture becomes a little sticky and starts to pull away from the sides of the pan. Remove from the heat, let cool for 2 minutes, then add the marshmallows and stir for 2 to 3 minutes, until the marshmallows melt. Stir in the vanilla, then quickly stir in the chocolate chips and nuts until the chocolate chips are melted but not completely incorporated (so you can still see some of the white) with some swirly streaks of black on white remaining. Immediately pour the mixture into the prepared pan and smooth the top with a spatula or your hands. Press some chips into the top of the fudge. Refrigerate until set, about 2 hours. Remove from the refrigerator, pull by the foil overhang to remove the fudge from the pan, and place the fudge on a cutting board. Cut into 36 squares. Store in a container at room temperature if you like your fudge soft; refrigerate if you like a firmer fudge.

LITCHFIELD
CORRECTIONAL
INSTITUTION

NAME: WARREN   SUZANNE
          LAST   FIRST

ALIAS: Crazy Eyes

NUMBER: 1103-1602   SEX: F   RACE: Black

NCIC NUMBER

LEAVE BLANK

FINGER PRINT CLASSIFICATION

RIGHT HAND

| Index | Middle | Ring | Little |

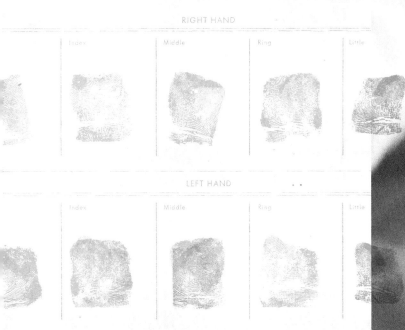

LEFT HAND

| Index | Middle | Ring | Little |

LARRY'S MOM'S

RUGELACH

BY AMY KANTER-BLOOM

My Larry would run home from grade school for the first night of Hanukkah and hope my back was turned so he could grab some rugelach. I'd smack his grubby little hands, then pull him in for a hug and say, "Not until after we say the blessings, Bubbala." He'll tell you he stopped doing that after the fifth grade but it was actually when he got his first girlfriend in high school. Don't tell him I told you. He'd kill me. "The Walking Embarrassment" is what he used to call me. He was a moody teen, but words still hurt. I'll never forget when he brought the aforementioned first girlfriend over for Shabbos dinner and she wouldn't try any of my rugelach. As soon as she left, I said, "No good, this one." And that was the last we saw of her.

MAKES 4 DOZEN COOKIES

DOUGH

- 2 cups (250 g) all-purpose flour
- ½ teaspoon salt
- 1 cup (225 g/2 sticks) unsalted butter, softened
- ¾ cup (180 ml) sour cream, at room temperature
- 1 large egg yolk

FILLING

- ½ cup (100 g) sugar
- 1 teaspoon ground cinnamon
- ½ cup (55 g) chopped toasted walnuts
- About 1½ cups (300 g) mini chocolate chips or currants
- 1 large egg
- 1 tablespoon milk

MAKE THE DOUGH:

In a large bowl, whisk together the flour and salt. In the bowl of a mixer fitted with the paddle attachment, combine the butter and sour cream and beat until smooth. Beat in the egg yolk, then slowly mix in the flour until a soft dough forms. Give the dough a knead or two if it needs help coming together, but don't overwork it. Form the dough into three equal-size balls, flatten the balls into approximately 1-inch (2.5-cm) disks, dust them with flour, and wrap each disk in plastic wrap. Refrigerate for at least 1 hour, until firm but still pliable. You can make the dough a day ahead (if rolling more than 1 hour ahead of time, remove the dough from the refrigerator a few minutes before rolling).

MAKE THE FILLING:

In a food processor, combine the sugar, cinnamon, and walnuts and pulse until the walnuts are finely ground.

ROLL AND FILL THE COOKIES:

Line two baking sheets with parchment paper or silicone mats.

Dust a work surface with flour and remove one piece of dough from the refrigerator, leaving the others refrigerated until you're ready to roll them. Using a floured rolling pin, roll the dough piece into a circle ⅛ inch (6 mm) thick and about 12 inches (30 cm) in diameter. Sprinkle about one third of the filling on top of the dough and press it lightly into the dough using the rolling pin. Using a paring knife or pizza wheel, cut the circle into sixteen equal wedges, first cutting the

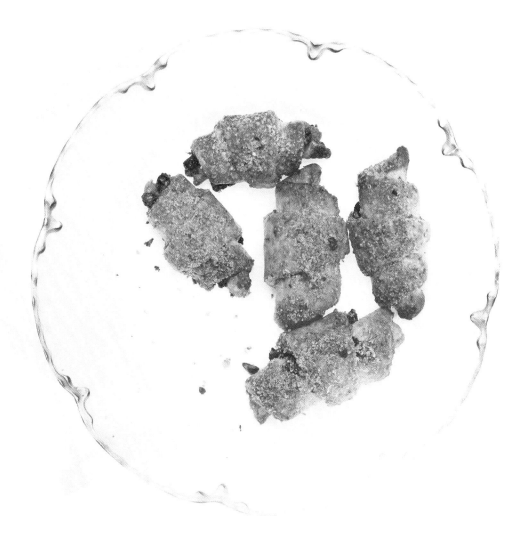

circle into quarters, then cutting each quarter into quarters. Sprinkle each wedge with chocolate chips, leaving a little space at the narrow tip and along the sides of the triangle. Starting with the wide edge, roll up each wedge and place the cookies, seam side down, on one of the prepared baking sheets. Tuck in the edges. Repeat with the remaining dough disks and filling (reserve any leftover filling for sprinkling on top of the cookies), placing them on the second cookie sheet. Refrigerate the baking sheets for 30 minutes.

BAKE THE COOKIES:

Meanwhile, position oven racks in the middle and lower third of the oven and preheat the oven to 375°F (190°C). In a small bowl, beat together the egg and milk to make an egg wash.

Remove the baking sheets from the refrigerator and brush each cookie with the egg wash. If any filling was left over, sprinkle it over the cookies. Bake for 20 to 30 minutes, switching the positions of the sheets halfway through baking, until lightly browned on top. Remove to wire racks and let cool completely. Store in airtight containers for up to 1 week.

TAYSTEE'S READING LIST

* *

Sinful Chocolate by Adrianne Byrd

Alice's Adventures in Wonderland by Lewis Carroll

Save Me a Seat by Rhea Kohan

Outlander by Diana Gabaldon

Fifty Shades of Grey by E.L. James

Do It Yourself Relationship Astrology by Lyn Birkbeck

101 Great Answers to the Toughest Interview Questions by Ron Fry

Riding the Iron Rooster by Paul Theroux

The Longest Ride by Nicholas Sparks

Seized by Jaid Black

Big Spankable Asses by Angie Daniels et al.

Destiny's Slaves by Marilyn Lee

Freshman Year and Other Unnatural Disasters by Meredith Zeitlin

Random Family by Adrian Nicole LeBlanc

This Is Where I Leave You by Jonathan Tropper

* * * *

"Books do not pay the rent, girl. Books do not

Bourguignon the beef."

—VEE

NAME........ PELAGE   CLAUDETTE
              LAST   FIRST

NUMBER........ 1011-3636   SEX........ F   RACE........ Black

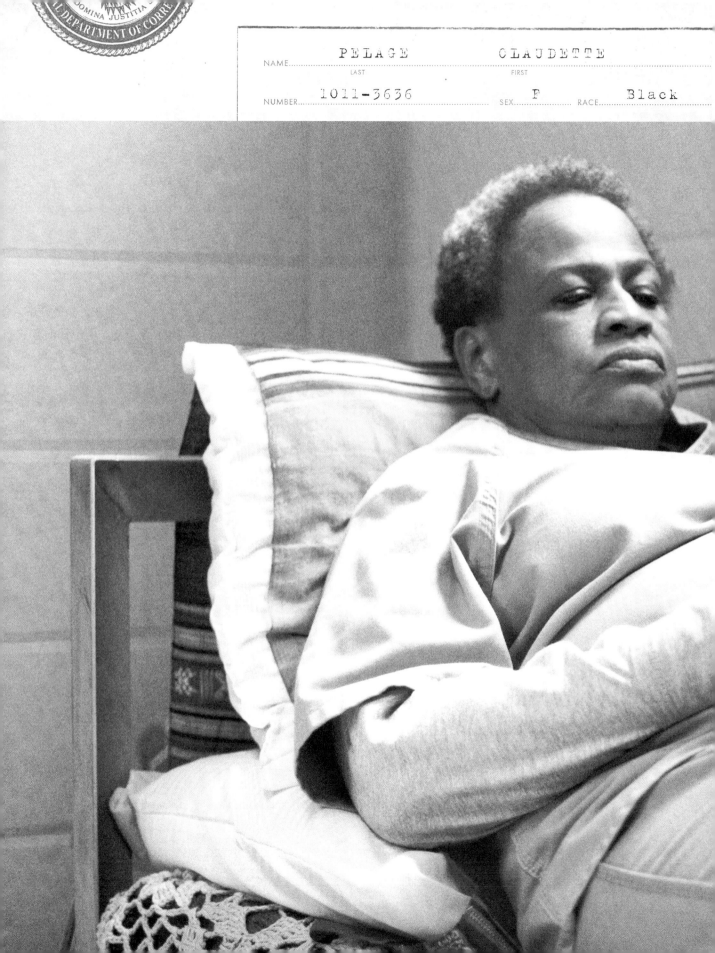

MISS CLAUDETTE'S EASTER CAKE

BY . . . . CLAUDETTE "MISS CLAUDETTE" PELAGE

Even in Litchfield, the end of Lent is a joyous time. I remember rara processions in the streets of Port-au-Prince. Furious dancing to the music of trumpets, drums and maracas, even hub caps, anything that made a beat. But we were good girls who listened from inside, our best Good Friday outfits carefully ironed the night before. In the morning, my mother would cover her cake in wrapping and I would walk in front of her through the streets on the way to church protecting her creation. We would sit calmly during the long Mass. Finally, afterward in the yard outside, my mother would proudly reveal her cake, cutting it into small pieces for everyone to try. We had to wait till all the others had eaten, and if I was lucky, there was a piece for me. It was the happiest time of my life.

MAKES . . . . ONE 9-INCH (23-CM) LAYER CAKE

INGREDIENTS

COCONUT CAKE

Butter for the pans, optional

2¼ cups (280 g) all-purpose flour

1 tablespoon baking powder

½ teaspoon salt

½ cup (1 stick; 115 g) unsalted butter, softened

1½ cups (375 g) sugar

3 large eggs

1 tablespoon pure Mexican vanilla (see Note)

1 teaspoon coconut extract

1¼ cups (300 ml) whole milk

1 cup (100 g) sweetened coconut flakes

(continued)

INSTRUCTIONS

MAKE THE COCONUT CAKE:

Preheat the oven to 350°F (175°C) and position an oven rack in the middle. Grease the bottom and sides of two 9-inch (23-cm) square or round baking pans with butter and line the pans with waxed paper or parchment paper.

Put the flour in a large bowl and whisk in the baking powder and salt. In the bowl of a mixer, beat the butter with the sugar until light and fluffy, about 3 minutes, starting at low speed and increasing to medium-high, then lower the speed to medium and add the eggs one at a time, beating well after each addition. Beat in the vanilla and coconut extracts.

Add the flour mixture in 3 additions, alternating each addition with one third of the milk, until fully blended. Fold in the coconut flakes.

Pour into the prepared pan and bake for 25 to 30 minutes, until the top springs back slightly when pressed and a tester inserted into the middle comes out clean. Let cool on wire racks for 15 minutes, then flip the pans over onto the racks and let cool completely.

INGREDIENTS

INSTRUCTIONS

COCONUT WHIPPED FROSTING

1½ cups (360 ml) heavy cream, chilled

½ cup (120 ml) canned coconut cream, chilled (shake the can well before chilling)

Pinch of salt

2 teaspoons pure Mexican vanilla extract (see Note)

FINISHING

1½ cups (200 g) sweetened coconut flakes

MAKE THE COCONUT WHIPPED FROSTING:

If space allows (walk-in prison kitchen freezer ideal), place the metal bowl from the electric mixer and the whisk attachment in the freezer for about 10 minutes or in the refrigerator for about 30 minutes.

Combine the heavy cream, coconut cream, and salt in the chilled mixing bowl and beat, starting at low speed and gradually increasing the speed to medium-high, until the cream just starts to thicken. Reduce the speed to medium and beat until soft peaks form. Add the vanilla and beat until stiff peaks form.

Arrange a cooled cake layer on a plate, cover with frosting, top with the second layer, and cover the top and sides of the cake with the frosting. Press the coconut flakes all over the top and sides. Slice and serve.

NOTE:

Much of the vanilla sold in Mexico is synthetic. How to tell? Fake Mexican vanilla is either clear or quite dark and super-cheap; it may be flavored by coumarin, an extract of the tonka bean that smells just like a super-charged vanilla but can cause liver damage (in the medical world it is used as an anticoagulant). Real Mexican vanilla is amber in color and translucent and the very best in flavor; the price tag is high, but Miss Claudette swears by it.

MARIA'S VALENTINE'S DAY COOKIES

BY . . . .

MARIA RUIZ

We didn't celebrate Valentine's when I was a kid. At least it's kind of nice that we get to celebrate in the joint. You see, my stepdad Chen Dong didn't grow up with it. But everyone at school was all about it. The teachers forced us to make red and pink paper hearts for everyone so nobody would feel left out. But you could tell how much someone liked you if they put work into it. There was a real hard boy they held back a year for skipping classes and smoking on school property. All the girls worked really hard on their hearts for him. But I baked a chocolate cookie at home in the shape of my chichis. Put some red sprinkles on and left it in his locker. After that he was all about me. Never paid any attention to those other girls after a taste of my cookie.

MAKES . . . .

ABOUT 4 DOZEN 2½-INCH (6-CM) HEART-SHAPED COOKIES

INGREDIENTS

COOKIES

1½ cups (190 g) all-purpose flour

½ cup (45 g) unsweetened cocoa powder

½ teaspoon baking powder

½ teaspoon baking soda

¼ teaspoon salt

½ cup (1 stick; 115 g) unsalted butter, softened

1 cup (200 g) sugar

1 large egg, at room temperature

1 large egg yolk, at room temperature

1 teaspoon vanilla extract

(continued)

INSTRUCTIONS

MAKE THE COOKIES:

In a medium bowl, whisk together the flour, cocoa powder, baking powder, baking soda, and salt.

In the bowl of a mixer fitted with the paddle attachment, beat together the butter and sugar on medium speed until pale and fluffy, about 3 minutes. Add the whole egg and egg yolk and beat until blended in, then beat in the vanilla. Reduce the speed to low, add the flour mixture, and mix just until the dough comes together. Gather the dough into a ball, divide it in half, and wrap each piece in plastic wrap; refrigerate until firm, at least 2 hours or up to 2 days (if making in advance, let stand at room temperature for 30 minutes before rolling).

Preheat the oven to 350°F (175°C) and position an oven rack in the middle. Line two baking sheets with parchment paper or silicone mats.

Take out one ball of dough, place it between two sheets of waxed paper, and using a rolling pin roll it out ⅛ inch (3 mm) thick. Cut out cookies with a

MARIA'S VALENTINE'S DAY COOKIES   (cont.)

RECIPE . . . .

INGREDIENTS

INSTRUCTIONS

ICING

1½ cups (185 g) confectioners' sugar

About ½ cup (100 g) crushed cinnamon candies (see Note), such as Red Hots or red-colored sugar or sprinkles

SPECIAL EQUIPMENT:

4-inch (10-cm) heart-shaped cookie cutter (measured at the widest curves of the heart)

2½-inch (6-cm) heart-shaped cookie cutter until you've used up all the dough; use a spatula to peel away excess dough and transfer the cookies to the prepared baking sheets. Gather up the scraps. Repeat with the second piece of dough. Combine the scraps from the two batches, re-roll once more, and cut out more cookies in the same manner. Discard the scraps.

Bake one sheet at a time until the cookies are firm on top and slightly darker around the edges, about 15 minutes. Let cool for 5 minutes on the baking sheets, then transfer to a wire rack to cool completely.

MAKE THE ICING:

In a medium bowl, whisk together the confectioners' sugar and 1½ tablespoons water until smooth; add a little more water ½ teaspoon at a time if the mixture isn't quite drizzling consistency. Spoon the icing into a pastry bag (or make an impromptu pastry bag out of a plastic storage bag; fill the bag and snip the end off for piping) and pipe the icing over a cookie in a zig-zag pattern. Immediately sprinkle the icing with candy pieces and lightly press them into the icing. Repeat with the remaining cookies. Let the icing set completely, about 1 hour, before eating. Store the cookies between sheets of waxed paper in an airtight container for up to 2 weeks.

NOTE:

To crush candies, place them in a heavy-duty zip-top bag and run a rolling pin over them.

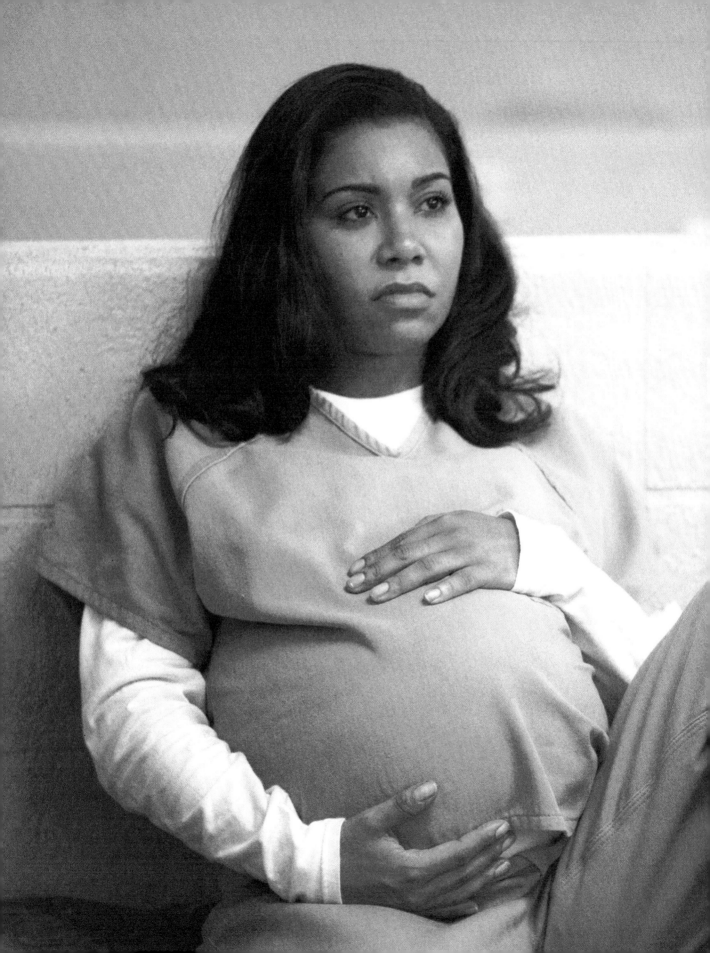

LITCHFIELD
CORRECTIONAL
INSTITUTION

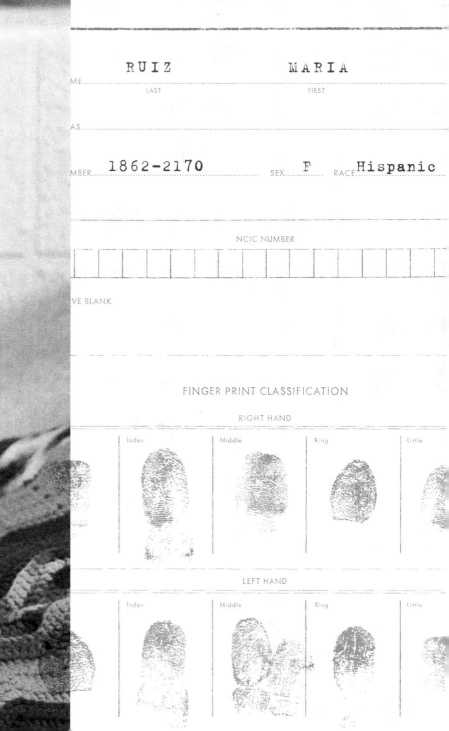

ME .... RUIZ   MARIA
              LAST   FIRST

AS ....

MBER 1862-2170   SEX ..... F ..... RACE Hispanic

NCIC NUMBER

VE BLANK

FINGER PRINT CLASSIFICATION

RIGHT HAND

| Index | Middle | Ring | Little |

LEFT HAND

| Index | Middle | Ring | Little |

CONTRABAND CANDY BAR BROWNIES

JOEL LUSCHEK
BY

I was at a party in high school once and my friend came by with a plate of brownies. I took one and chowed down, 'cause why not? It was only after I ate the whole thing that he revealed they were a very special kind of brownie. Having never had one of those kind before, I freaked out for about five minutes, wondering if I would die. Then I just got back to drinking. It didn't kick in until a few hours later when I stood up to go to the bathroom. My head was light, and I didn't know what was going on, but my friend did. He ran to the kitchen and came back with a piece of bread. "Eat this," he said. I started to chew and couldn't even comprehend what I was really doing. "What does it feel like," he asked. I said, "Like little bread planets are orbiting my tongue sun." He laughed and then we watched The Who's Tommy on Turner Classic Movies. Oh, normal brownies? What more can I say? I like brownies, even when they're just being served up as a treat in the caf. They're still delicious.

MAKES..... 16 BROWNIES

INGREDIENTS

Nonstick cooking spray

3 ounces (85 g) unsweetened chocolate, chopped

½ cup (1 stick; 115 g) unsalted butter, cut into chunks

1 cup (200 g) sugar

½ teaspoon baking powder

¼ teaspoon salt

2 large eggs

1 teaspoon vanilla extract

⅔ cup (85 g) all-purpose flour

About 20 Milky Way or Snickers bites, cut in half

INSTRUCTIONS

Preheat the oven to 350°F (175°C) and position an oven rack in the middle. Line an 8-inch (20-cm) baking dish with foil so that it extends up the sides and over the edges of the pan. Coat the foil with nonstick cooking spray.

Put the chocolate and butter in a small bowl set over a pan of simmering water and stir until melted. Remove from the heat and let cool.

In a medium bowl, whisk together the sugar, baking powder, and salt, then whisk in the eggs and vanilla until combined. Whisk in the melted chocolate mixture until smooth. Stir in the flour until completely incorporated and no white streaks remain.

Pour half of the batter evenly into the prepared pan. Arrange the candy bar pieces on top of the batter cut side down, leaving a little space between them and along the sides of the pan, then scrape the remaining half of the batter out of the bowl and into the pan to cover the candy. Smooth the surface.

(continued)

CONTRABAND CANDY BAR BROWNIES (cont.)

INGREDIENTS

INSTRUCTIONS

Place the pan in the oven and bake until the top of the brownie is set and the edges have pulled away from the sides of the pan, about 25 minutes (see Note). Let cool on a wire rack for at least 1 hour. Lift the brownies from the pan using the extended foil edges and place on a cutting board. Slide the foil out from underneath and cut the brownies into 2-inch (5-cm) squares. The brownies can be stored in an airtight container for up to 1 week.

NOTE:

The usual stick-in-a-toothpick-to-check-for-done-ness technique isn't recommended here, as it's invalidated if your pick hits a spot of candy bar.

WARNING:
DISCONNECT DISHWASHER
POWER SUPPLY
BEFORE CLEANING.

HOBART

CRAZY EYES'S EXPLODING STRAWBERRY PIE

BY..... SUZANNE WARREN

When I was eleven and three quarters Mom and Dad took Gracie and me to the circus. It was in a big colorful tent down by 4th and Massachusetts in an abandoned parking lot. That was before they rezoned the area for mixed-used development. At the entrance to the tent a man on stilts took our tickets and pointed us toward the seats. We were only a few rows from the back, where it was dark once the show started. First there was music. Then there were clowns. Lots of clowns. They were the wild kind, popping up in the middle of the audience. One pulled down a man's pants and showed his underwear. Suddenly the spotlight came on next to me, and a clown jumped up in front of us. He had a big sad frown painted on his face, but he was smiling. He took out a pie and slapped Dad in the face. Mom was in shock and Gracie started crying. I thought it was hilarious. Now I love the circus.

MAKES.... **ONE 9-INCH PIE**

INGREDIENTS

1½ quarts (860 g) fresh strawberries, hulled

1 cup (200 g) sugar

¼ cup (30 g) cornstarch

Pinch of salt

2 tablespoons fresh lemon juice

3 tablespoons unsalted butter, cut into bits

One 9-inch (23-cm) baked piecrust, store-bought or homemade (recipe follows)

INSTRUCTIONS

Put 2 cups (286 g) of the strawberries in a blender or food processor and blend until pureed. Cut the remaining strawberries in half if they are large; otherwise leave them whole.

In a medium saucepan, combine the sugar, cornstarch, and salt. Whisk in ½ cup (120 ml) water, then add the pureed strawberries, followed by the lemon juice and butter. Place over medium-high heat and bring to a simmer; simmer for 2 to 3 minutes, until thickened, slightly glossy, and a shade darker.

Arrange 2 cups (286 g) of the uncooked strawberries in the bottom of the baked piecrust and pour half of the cooked berries over them; shake the pan to evenly coat the uncooked strawberries. Arrange the remaining 2 cups (286 g) uncooked strawberries on top and cover with the remaining cooked berries; shake the pan again to make an even layer. Let cool to room temperature, then refrigerate for 4 to 6 hours to set before serving (or throwing).

BUTTERY PIECRUST

RECIPE . . . .

This crust can be used in any recipe that calls for a prebaked piecrust.

MAKES TWO 9-INCH (23-CM) PIECRUSTS

INGREDIENTS

2½ cups (310 g) unbleached all-purpose flour

1 teaspoon salt

1 cup (2 sticks; 225 g) unsalted butter, cut into ¼-inch (6-mm) bits

¼ to ½ cup (60 to 120 ml) ice-cold water

INSTRUCTIONS

In a large bowl, whisk together the flour and salt. Cut the butter into the dry ingredients using a pastry blender or pastry fork until most of the butter is the consistency of coarse crumbs with some larger, pea-size pieces remaining. Drizzle ¼ cup (60 ml) ice water over the mixture and toss with a fork to moisten the dough evenly. Press down on the dough with your hand; if the bits of dough stick together, you're good to go. If not, drizzle on another tablespoon of water and cut the water in with the fork again. Repeat until the dough sticks together easily but is not overly moist.

Divide the dough in half and press each half into a flat disk. Wrap each disk tightly in plastic wrap and refrigerate for at least 30 minutes or up to a day. (You will have dough remaining for an extra piecrust; place the second disk in a freezer bag and keep it frozen for up to 6 months; defrost completely before rolling it out.)

Flour a clean work surface and a rolling pin. Unwrap one piece of dough and place it on the floured surface. Roll the dough into a circle 12 to 13 inches (30 to 33 cm) in diameter, rolling from the center outward, the fewer strokes the better for the most tender crust. Roll your dough loosely around the rolling pin or fold it into quarters and arrange it in a 9-inch (23-cm) pie pan, pressing the dough into the bottom and the corners of the pan and patching any holes or cracks with dough scraps. Tuck the overhanging dough underneath itself and lay the rim on the lip of the pie pan. Crimp the dough by pressing it all around with the tines of a fork. Refrigerate the rolled-out dough for at least 30 minutes or overnight.

(continued)

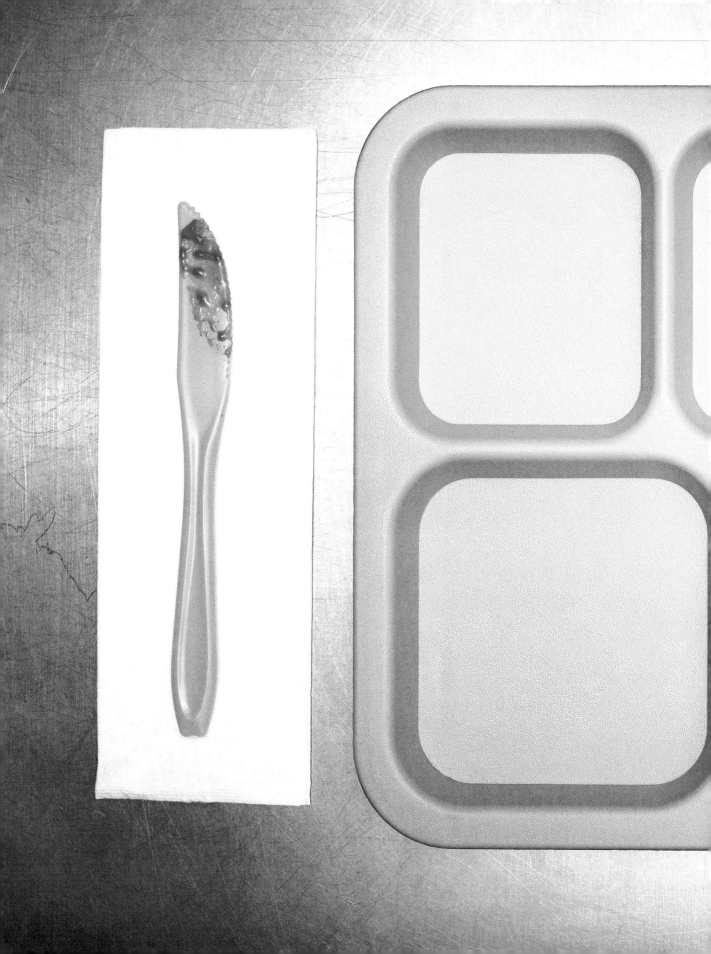

CRAZY EYES'S EXPLODING STRAWBERRY PIE (cont.)

RECIPE

INGREDIENTS

INSTRUCTIONS

Preheat the oven to 400°F (200°C). Place a sheet of foil, shiny side down, in the bottom and sides of the crust (this keeps it from browning too much). Fill the crust with pie weights or uncooked beans. Bake for 20 minutes, then remove the foil with the weights. Prick the crust with a fork all over, return the crust to the oven, and bake for another 5 to 10 minutes, until the crust is golden brown. Remove from the oven, place on a wire rack, and let cool completely before filling.

POST-PRISON VARIATION

STRAWBERRY ORANGE PIE: Substitute orange juice for the water and add 1 tablespoon Cointreau or Grand Marnier to the filling as you cook it. Use farmers' market fresh strawberries, sprinkle a little fresh orange zest or minced candied orange peel on top, and finish with a dollop of crème fraîche. And, of course, make your own buttery piecrust using the recipe on page 215.

"I t   or you!"

INDEX

* *

TO THE WHOLE ORANGE FAMILY,
all of whom are juicy and delicious.